T0238461

BestMasters

Springer awards „BestMasters" to the best master's theses which have been completed at renowned universities in Germany, Austria, and Switzerland.

The studies received highest marks and were recommended for publication by supervisors. They address current issues from various fields of research in natural sciences, psychology, technology, and economics.

The series addresses practitioners as well as scientists and, in particular, offers guidance for early stage researchers.

Susanne Göbel

A Polynomial Translation of Mobile Ambients into Safe Petri Nets

Understanding a Calculus of Hierarchical Protection Domains

Springer Vieweg

Susanne Göbel
Kaiserslautern, Germany

Best Master Thesis 2014 among German, Austrian and Swiss Computer Science Faculties awarded by their union (Fakultätentagspreis)

BestMasters
ISBN 978-3-658-11764-1   ISBN 978-3-658-11765-8 (eBook)
DOI 10.1007/978-3-658-11765-8

Library of Congress Control Number: 2015955835

Springer Vieweg
© Springer Fachmedien Wiesbaden 2016
This work is subject to copyright. All rights are reserved by the Publisher, whether the whole or part of the material is concerned, specifically the rights of translation, reprinting, reuse of illustrations, recitation, broadcasting, reproduction on microfilms or in any other physical way, and transmission or information storage and retrieval, electronic adaptation, computer software, or by similar or dissimilar methodology now known or hereafter developed.
The use of general descriptive names, registered names, trademarks, service marks, etc. in this publication does not imply, even in the absence of a specific statement, that such names are exempt from the relevant protective laws and regulations and therefore free for general use.
The publisher, the authors and the editors are safe to assume that the advice and information in this book are believed to be true and accurate at the date of publication. Neither the publisher nor the authors or the editors give a warranty, express or implied, with respect to the material contained herein or for any errors or omissions that may have been made.

Printed on acid-free paper

Springer Vieweg is a brand of Springer Fachmedien Wiesbaden
Springer Fachmedien Wiesbaden is part of Springer Science+Business Media
(www.springer.com)

Acknowledgements

Vielen Dank...

...möchte ich zunächst meinen beiden Betreuern Roland Meyer und Reiner Hüchting sagen, für Betreuung und Unterstützung, die schon lange vor dieser Arbeit begonnen hat und sich hoffentlich auch noch lange fortsetzen wird. Ihr habt mir ein faszinierendes Feld der Informatik erschlossen, dass mich hoffentlich irgendwann ernähren, auf jeden Fall aber nie loslassen wird.

Mit der Masterarbeit schließt sich ein spannendes Lebenskapitel: Mein Studium. Ich habe Freiheit in einem Maß erfahren, dass ich vorher kaum für möglich gehalten hätte, aber auch Heimweh und Verlorensein. Ich danke meinen Eltern und Großeltern für Geborgenheit und einen Ort, an den ich bis heute fliehen kann, wenn mir alles zuviel wird. Ihr habt mir mein Studium ermöglicht und ihr seid bis heute für mich da, wenn ich Sorgen habe.

Genauso begleitet haben mich Freundinnen, die schon in der Schulzeit an meiner Seite waren und bis heute sind: Sonja, die vom Kindergarten bis als Trauzeugin mit mir gegangen ist, Mara, die mit mir die Männerwelt unsicher gemacht hat und bei Liebeskummer immer eine zuverlässige Anlaufstelle war, Marina, die mich nicht erst, aber vor allem in meiner Schwangerschaft so kompetent und mitfühlend begleitet hat und bestimmt mal eine tolle Ärztin wird, Kristina, mit der man schon immer wunderbar träumen und spielen konnte, und schließlich Vali, die alle Sorgen einfach weglacht. Noch länger mit mir geht meine Schwester: Wir haben uns gemeinsam durch Pubertät und Schule gekämpft und so viel zusammen erlebt, wie man nur als Geschwister kann. So verschieden sich unsere Leben entwickelt haben, das Band ist doch nie ganz abgerissen. Ich bin unglaublich stolz und glücklich, euch alle zu haben – ich hab euch lieb.

Während des Studiums habe ich neue Freunde gefunden, auch wenn die erste Clique nicht gehalten hat, bin ich doch euch allen dankbar für die gemeinsame Zeit. Viele sind geblieben und sind zu wichtigen RatgeberInnen, LeidensgenossInnen und in Helens Fall sogar beinahe zu einem Familienmitglied geworden. Da sind noch Anne, Frank, Laura und Stephan, Lars, Marco, Christian, Roya und Christina. Mit manchen kann man schwimmen gehen, mit manchen wandern, Brettspiele spielen oder Musik machen, aber mit allen kann man reden.

Ebenfalls dankbar bin ich der Studienstiftung und Professor Liggesmeyer, der mich im zweiten Semester vorgeschlagen hat. Ich habe durch sie den Zugang zu einem Gesellschaftsbereich erhalten, der sich sicherlich im Berufsleben als hilfreich erweisen wird. Dem gesamten Fachbereich, vor allem der Fachschaft und den Gremien danke ich für unsere gemeinsame Zeit und Arbeit. Ich denke, wir haben viel bewegt und ich bin sicher, ich habe viel gelernt.

Ganz neben der Uni und dennoch eng damit verwoben ist mein Mann Chris, der seit drei Jahren mit mir durch dick und dünn geht. Für eine Ehe, die so ist, wie sie sein sollte, weil sie uns beide trägt und stützt, für eine Schulter, an die ich mich immer lehnen kann, auch wenn sie eher spitz und etwas härter ist, möchte ich dir aus tiefstem Herzen danken. Du hast dich begeistert mit mir in das Abenteuer Familie gestürzt und bist so liebevoll und fürsorglich bisher für mich und jetzt für Katharina und mich da.

Schließlich sind da noch Mady und Katharinas Patentante Natalie, die uns durch die schwere Zeit des Krankenhauses begleitet haben und hoffentlich auch weiterhin als selbstgewählte Familie mit uns zusammenstehen.

Und dann, ja dann ist da natürlich noch die kleine Katharina selbst, die nicht erst seit dem 20.8.2013 unser Leben ordentlich durcheinanderwirbelt. Ich danke dir fürs Kuscheln, für dein Lächeln und das unfassbare Vertrauen, das aus deinen großen blauen Augen spricht. Du bist so ruhig und friedlich, dass ich die letzten Kapitel fertigstellen konnte, als du schon in meinen Armen lagst.

Kaiserslautern im Dezember 2013

Contents

List of Figures

Chapter 1
Background

We start by introducing the related literature on both the Mobile Ambient (MA) calculus and its ancestor the π-calculus. Both calculi are Turing-complete in general form so that reachability is undecidable. Still, many results exist that prove reachability for restricted subclasses but most of these classes for MA are syntactically restricted so that certain language constructs are excluded.

This work derives a translation of the complete MA calculus into one-safe Petri nets that yields a finite net if and only if the original MA process is bounded. This purely semantically restricted translation leaves us with full expressiveness but guarantees a P-SPACE-complete decision of reachability on all finite MA processes. We devote this chapter to a short introduction of the general translation idea, its context in existing literature and the recapitulation of the necessary definitions.

1.1 Introduction and Related Work

Since its development in 1998 in [CG98] the Mobile Ambient (MA) calculus has received a lot of attention. It allows for the specification of hierarchical protection domains like firewalls around a concurrency framework close to that of the π-calculus ([Mil99], [SW01]). The need to abstract such systems arises in the verification of security properties for mobile devices [UAUC10] where model checking is automated using the MA calculus but also in the area of architecture description languages ([Oqu04]).

The pure MA calculus, also called mobility calculus, comes unlike its ancestor, the π-calculus, without any communication primitives. Still, it is already Turing-complete [CG98]. A lot of variations and extensions have been proposed, e.g. Safe Ambients [LS03], also enriched with passwords [MH02] where the capabilities are only executed if both participants agree, or the Controlled Ambient Calculus [TZH02] which focusses on security modeling. The MA founders' subsequent work like [GC03] uses the calculus enriched with communication which then also allows for the convenient encoding of the asynchronous π-calculus [CG98]. The Ambient logic [CG00] opens the way for conventional model checking. Already the introductary paper proves decidability of the model checking problem between a subclass of the ambient calculus and a subclass of the Ambient logic. Later, PSPACE-completeness was shown in [CZG⁺01].

Just like ourselves, [BZ09] searches for fragments of the MA calculus for which verification's premier problem, reachability, is still decidable. Therefore they investigate syntactic restrictions removing the *open* capability and the restriction as well as allowing for guarded replication only. However, their investigated fragments are still Turing-complete as shown by [MP05].

We will enable efficient verification for a purely semantically restricted subclass of the MA calculus by an encoding into Safe Petri nets. Safe Petri nets [RT86] offer PSPACE-complete reachability, liveness, and persistence analysis ([EN94], [CEP95]) combined with high expressiveness. The encoding of Safe Petri nets into Boolean formulas allows for the use of SAT solvers. Techniques like bounded model checking [OTK04] can increase their efficiency by avoiding the state explosion problem [Val98]. Thus, Safe Petri nets are a popular framework for verification.

To our knowledge, they haven't been employed yet to directly encode fragments of the MA calculus, though. Still, [KK06] uses arbitrary p/t Petri nets to approximate graph rewriting systems for counter-example based verification. The MA and the π-calculus are mentioned as typical graph rewriting systems to model mobile processes. As we will highlight, MA is even a tree rewriting system.

[RVMS12] contribute to the verification of depth bounded processes with restrictions (into which the depth bounded MA calculus falls) by the introduction of ν-MSR. It allows for a convenient encoding of name binding since it comes with an own restriction operator. While their approach guarantees decidability of termination, boundedness and coverability for any depth bounded MA process the decision procedure is known to not be primitively recursive. We will introduce a depth and breadth bounded fragment of the MA calculus in which we cannot only decide reachability but even with a P-SPACE upper bound.

There are a lot of verification results for the MA inspirer, the π-calculus, which rely on the notion of depth bounded processes introduced by [Mey08]. While termination [Mey08] and coverability [WZH10] are still decidable for these systems, reachability is undecidable in general. We are especially interested in the subclasses of depth bounded processes for which encodings into Petri nets have been proposed. Employing the decidable Petri net reachability all those classes have a decidable reachability problem. Still, the decision procedure may have large complexity depending on the class of Petri nets used for the encoding and the size of the encoding itself. [Mey09] introduces the huge fragment of structurally stationary π-calculus processes giving a translation into p/t Petri nets which can become non-primitively recursive. [MG09] extends this class further to mixed bounded processes again by an encoding into p/t Petri nets.

For Finite Control Processes (FCP) [Dam96], which form a subclass of structurally stationary processes, encodings into bounded Petri nets have been proposed: [MKS08] gave an exponential encoding of FCPs into bounded Petri nets, identifying a subclass for which the translation already produced a safe net. Recently, this work has been refined by [MKH12] who could present a polynomial encoding for arbitrary FCPs into Safe Petri nets. Although one can suspect that our translation closely matches their work we will see that the different ways to deal with restricted names enforce quite different translation mechanisms.

While the send and receive actions in the π-calculus allow for an almost arbitrary runtime-spread of a name, MA has no name passing mechanism so that the spread of a name can be characterised by some static properties.We determine the relevant positions via a generic pre-processing of MA equations. The additional syntax to mark the positions requires an intermediate calculus which we call rMA. It extends the MA calculus in a sense that does not modify its behaviour as we show via a bismulation. The translation of rMA terms into safe Petri nets manages all relations by unique names. The generated Petri net is thus finite if and only if the number of names used in parallel is bounded. This characterises a bounded process as we show. The usage of a substitution net further improves our construction for the bounded case by guaranteeing it to be polynomial in porcess size and bounds. Since deciding reachability in safe Petri nets is PSPACE-complete, we get a PSPACE-complete decision for bounded MA processes as well.

1.2 Preliminaries

We introduce the two formalisms our translation links, namely Safe Petri nets and Mobile Ambient processes, and the proof mechanism of bisimulations which we use to prove the link between the systems. We emphasise the graphical system notation that increases readability of this work as well as understandability.

1.2.1 Safe Petri Nets

A Petri net is a tuple (P, T, F, M_0) where P and T are the disjoint sets of places and transitions, respectively, $F \subseteq (P \times T) \cup (T \times P)$ is the flow relation, and $M_0 = \mathbb{N}^{|P|}$ is the initial marking. Each marking is specified as a vector representing the current number of tokens per place. We use the standard graphical representation with nodes represented as circles, their current token count as dots, transitions as rectangles, and the flow between them as arcs.

Petri nets are commonly used to express system behaviour. Often, the tokens are understood as threads which execute commands in the program part symbolised by their surrounding place. Thus, transitions model possible control transfer.

Example 1.1 (Client-server application modeled with a Petri net).

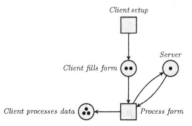

Fig. 1.1 Interplay of a server with an arbitrary number of clients (one token per client).

The size of a net $N = (P, T, F, M_0)$ is $|N| = |P| + |T| + \sum_{p \in P}(\sum_{t \in T}(|F(p,t)| + |F(t,p)|)) + \sum_{p \in P} M_0(p)$. A transition t is enabled on a marking M if the places from which the transition takes tokens $(F(*,t))$ contain at least as many tokens as the transition wants to take. A marking M is called reachable in the net N if there is a sequence of enabled transitions which transforms M_0 into M.

Petri nets only fulfilling these restrictions are usually called p/t Petri nets to distinguish them from their bounded subclasses. A net is called k-bounded if no place in any reachable marking contains more than k tokens. One-bounded nets are called safe. They have excellent model checking properties: The reachability problem is only PSPACE-complete for Safe Petri nets while it is already EXSPACE-hard for arbitrary Petri nets [EN94].

1.2.2 Mobile Ambients

The Mobile Ambient (MA) calculus focusses on the step-wise transition of processes or devices through administrative domains. These domains are called ambients and each one possesses a name n. Their nesting forms a tree structure. They are entered, left or removed ("opened") via the execution of *capabilities* $\pi := \{in\ n,\ out\ n,\ open\ n\}$ on their name n.

Definition 1.2 (Syntax). P is a MA term if it is built according to the following rules: $P ::= 0 \mid \pi.P \mid n[P] \mid !P \mid \nu n.P \mid P|Q \mid K(\vec{a})$, where $\pi =\{$in n, out n, open n$\}$.

The ambient symbol $n[P]$ expresses that P is running within ambient n. As for the π-calculus 0 has no behaviour, $P|Q$ is the parallel composition of P and Q, $!P$ the replication of P, $K(\vec{a})$ the call to process identifier K with parameters $\vec{a}$ and νn. P is the restriction which introduces a new name n and limits its scope onto P. A name n occurring in the scope of a restriction νn is called restricted, otherwise called free. The congruence requires α-conversion of restricted names which we express by the name substitution $\sigma(n/l)$ that replaces each occurence of n in P by one of l but is only applicable if l did not exist in P before.

The $in\ n$ and $out\ n$ capabilities can move an ambient with all its children into or out of a sibling ambient n. The execution of $open\ n$ removes an ambient n so that its children now belong to n's former parent.

Definition 1.3 (Semantics: Structural Congruence). MA guarantees

Refl $P \equiv P$
Symm $P \equiv Q \Rightarrow Q \equiv P$
Trans $P \equiv Q, Q \equiv R \Rightarrow P \equiv R$
Pers $P \equiv Q \Rightarrow \nu n.P \equiv \nu n.Q,\ P|R \equiv Q|R,\ n[P] \equiv n[Q],\ \pi n.P \equiv \pi n.Q$

As for the π-calculus, $|$ and ν are commutative and associative, with ν also allowing for scope extrusion $(\nu n.(P\,|\,Q) \equiv (\nu n.P)\,|\,Q$ if n not free in $Q)$. The additional rules are:

$$\nu n.m[P] \equiv m[\nu n.P] \text{ if } n \neq m \qquad P|0 \equiv P \qquad \nu n.0 \equiv 0$$
$$\nu n.P \equiv \nu l.P\sigma(n/l) \qquad\qquad\qquad !P \equiv P\,|\,!P \qquad !0 \equiv 0$$

0 is understood as equivalent to the empty process $(0 \equiv \varepsilon)$.

A prefix π binds stronger than any other primitive, that is $\pi.P|Q \equiv (\pi.P)|Q$. Next comes the replication $!P$ so that we have $!P|Q \equiv (!P)|Q$. A restriction is still stronger than the parallel composition: $\nu n.P|Q \equiv (\nu n.P)|Q$. Each ambient's binding is explicitly stated by its closing bracket since we expect a correct bracket tree.

The transition relation specifies the possible actions giving a formal semantics to the execution of capabilities and calls. The MA calculus is a classical prefix system in which each action consumes exactly one prefix. Neither restrictions nor ambients are understood as prefixes. Therefore, the transition relation is independent of them. It further applies to complete congruence classes via $P \equiv P', P \rightsquigarrow Q, Q \equiv Q' \Rightarrow P' \rightsquigarrow Q'$.

Definition 1.4 (Semantics: Transition Relation). The transition relation defines the four actions:

call: $K(\vec{a}) \rightsquigarrow K_{\llcorner}\vec{a}/\vec{x}_{\lrcorner}$
in: $n[in\ m.P|Q]|m[R] \rightsquigarrow m[n[P|Q]|R]$
out: $m[n[out\ m.P|Q]|R] \rightsquigarrow n[P|Q]|m[R]$
open: $open\ m.P\,|\,m[Q] \rightsquigarrow P\,|\,Q$

It ignores neighbouring terms completely via $P \rightsquigarrow Q \Rightarrow P\,|\,R \rightsquigarrow Q\,|\,R$ and also ignores preceding terms as long as they do not contain prefixes: $P \rightsquigarrow Q \Rightarrow n[P] \rightsquigarrow n[Q]$, and $P \rightsquigarrow Q \Rightarrow \nu n.P \rightsquigarrow \nu n.Q$.

For the rest of this work we enforce that only those equations are defined in an MA process which are later used, and that the parameter list of each definition is restricted to the finally used parameters.

Definition 1.5 (MA process). Let $D = \bigcup_{i=1}^{n} D_{i\llcorner}\vec{x}_{i\lrcorner} := P_i$ a set of defining MA equations and I an MA term. The tuple (D, I) is called MA process if

minPara: For all D_i all $x_i \in \vec{x}_i$ occur in P_i.
    closed: All calls to process identifiers in any P_i are only done to elements of D.
    complete: Each call in $I \bigcup D$ happens to elements of D.
    reachable: Each D_i is either already called in I or in one of the D_j callable by I or its (recursive) callees.

In our complexity analysis it will be necessary to reason about the size of such an MA process. We define it according to the size of π-calculus terms and Safe Petri nets as the sum over all syntactic elements. Congruent process terms can have different sizes, for example $size(P|0) = size(P) + 1$. Since we use the process equations in their original form, it is important to use the original process's size for our reasoning rather than some congruent, smaller version.

To simplify matters and exclude pathological cases we restrict ourselves to processes in which restricted names and formal parameters occur only once per equation and are never also used as free names. Analogously to the π-calculus we call this property no clash (NC)[MKH12]. In fact, the original NC criterion was even stricter and forbid multiple restrictions of a name over all equations.

Definition 1.6 (NC). Let $A = (D, I)$ an MA process with $fn(A)$ all names occurring freely in D or I, $rn(A)$ the set of names occurring restricted in D or I, and $pn(A)$ all names occurring as formal parameters in D. A fulfills the no clash (NC) criterion if

1. The sets $fn(A)$, $rn(A)$, and $pn(A)$ are pairwisely disjoint.
2. A name is restricted at most once within an equation D_i and in I.
3. A name is used at most once within a formal parameter list.

Together with the restriction to specify only parameters which are later used (Definition 1.5 on the facing page) we make sure that each defining equation uses a parameter list that is as short as possible.

1.2.3 Bisimulations

Bisimulations link state transition systems which show the same behaviour to an external observer. A bisimulation cares for the action with which a state is transformed into another one. If there are several possible actions in a state, the bisimilar state should be able to perform an action leading into a new bisimilar state for each one of them.

To talk about behaviour, bisimulations use the abstraction of actions. The set Act of actions consists of all system actions Sys and of the waiting action ε. The system actions vary with the studied systems but can always be partitioned into modifying actions mod, that encode externally visible behaviour, and silent actions τ. The latter are simple prefix removals while the former have some further effect additionally to the prefix removal. For example, the system actions for the MA calculus are all steps according to $\leadsto$, i.e. $Sys_{MA} = \{call, in, out, open\}$ with $mod_{MA} = \{call, in, out, open\}$ and $\tau_{MA} = \emptyset$.

We will concentrate on weak bisimulations where one assumes that the external observer cannot witness silent actions. To abstract them away, we define a relaxed transition relation which allows arbitrarily many silent actions before and after exactly one action $\alpha \in Act$.

Definition 1.7 (Transition relation with silent actions). Let $\alpha \in Act$. $P_1 \Rightarrow^{\widehat{\alpha}} P_n$ iff

$$\exists P_i, P_j : P_1 \leadsto^{\tau^*} P_i \leadsto^{\alpha} P_j \leadsto^{\tau^*} P_n$$

The action α may of course also be a silent action ($\alpha \in \tau$) or even encode no step at all (ε). This new transition relation allows us to define the weak bisimulation:

Definition 1.8 (Weak bisimulation). A binary relation $S \subseteq \mathbb{P} \times \mathbb{P}$ over processes is a weak bismiula-tion iff $(P, Q) \in S$ implies for all actions $\alpha \in Act$

1. Whenever $P \leadsto^{\alpha} P'$, then for some $Q', Q \Rightarrow^{\widehat{\alpha}} Q'$ and $(P', Q') \in S$,
2. Whenever $Q \leadsto^{\alpha} Q'$, then for some $P'.P \Rightarrow^{\widehat{\alpha}} P'$ and $(P', Q') \in S$.

A process can mimic its bisimilar counterpart's behaviour. In every state it can do a transition for each action the bisimilar state can process. A weak bisimulation S can be visualised by two commutative simulation diagrams:

.

To abstract the concrete relation away and address bisimilarity as a property in general we give the following definition of weak bisimilarity.

Definition 1.9 (Weak bisimilarity). Two systems T_1 and T_2 are called weakly bisimilar ($T_1 \simeq T_2$) if a weak bisimulation exists between them.

In order to combine bisimulations we will make use of their transitivity.

Lemma 1.10 (Transitivity of weak bisimulations). *Let* $\mathcal{P}_x, \mathcal{P}_y$, *and* $\mathcal{P}_z$ *processes and* $S_1 \subseteq \mathcal{P}_x \times \mathcal{P}_y$ *and* $S_2 \subseteq \mathcal{P}_y \times \mathcal{P}_z$ *weak bisimulations. Then* $S_2 \circ S_1$ *is also a weak bisimulation.*

Proof. The proof can be found in [Mil89, p. 110]. $\square$

As discussed before the external observer cannot witness silent actions. Thus, a silent prefix τ does not influence a system's possible actions since it can be consumed before the required action α.

Lemma 1.11 (Silent actions). *Let* P *an arbitrary process.*

$$P \simeq \tau.P$$

Proof. The proof can be found in [Mil89, p. 111]. Roughly, $\tau.P$ executes τ before mimicking P's actual action to establish a simulation of P by $\tau.P$. In the opposite direction $\tau.P$ can only execute its silent action which P simply simulates by ε. $\square$

Chapter 2
Translating MA Processes into Safe Petri Nets — The Idea

The notion already developed in the original "Mobile Ambients"-paper [CG98, p. 144] that an MA process is a **tree** gives rise to the idea to use this tree as the data structure encoded into the Petri nets. We depict first MA trees in Section 2.1. Restrictions and ambients are inner nodes and all terms starting with a capability, replication, 0, or a call are leaves.

When we encode the capability actions into transitions in Section 2.2 the **locality of changes** in the MA calculus greatly helps. This property is only too natural when we consider MA's origin in fire wall modeling where each level must be step-wisely taken. It naturally fits into the Petri net world since only few and easily identifiable places are affected by each transition.

Based on the requirements of such a translation we propose an encoding into Petri net places which are named after all possible parent-child relations. We discuss problematic ambiguities which arise due to the management by name. They are resolved in Section 2.3 where we introduce two distinct name sets $\mathcal{A}$, which keeps the tree unambiguous, and $\mathcal{L}$, which allows us to drop the restrictions. We derive their management via additional Petri net transitions.

2.1 Translating MA Terms into Safe Petri Net Markings

Every MA process term can be represented as a tree where the inner node structure depicts the ambient hierarchy with the restrictions while the leaves are prefix guarded, that is each leaf starts with a capability π, is a call or 0, or a replication. The parallel compositions separate siblings.

Example 2.1 (Simple ambient hierarchies). The process $n[P|m[Q|R]]$ corresponds to the tree:

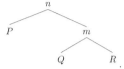

We do not wish to order a node's children in the tree but define it to represent all process terms congruent by the rule $P|Q \equiv Q|P$. Thus, the example tree above also stands for the process terms $n[P|m[R|Q]]$ $n[m[Q|R]|P]$ and $n[m[R|Q]|P]$. We will later abstract even more congruence rules away so that one marking represents an even larger subset of a process term's congruence class.

To maintain a tree rather than a forest if parallel compositions occur at the process's top level it is necessary to add an artificial root *root* adopting all so far orphaned process terms. We will always have this root as to prevent any process term from becoming an orphan but only depict it in figures if necessary to keep them representing a tree.

We use the Safe Petri net's places to represent all possible parent-child relations with the tokens representing the actual ones. E.g., a token on the place labeled $n \to m$ shows that an ambient n is a direct child of an ambient m whereas another token on $P \to m$ represents a similar relation between a (leaf) process term P and the ambient.

Example 2.2 (Translating a tree). The process term $m[P|n[\ldots]]$ represents the following tree which is then translated into a net marking:

Just like the tree it depicts the marking doesn't define an ordering on a node's children. Thus, each marking represents all processes modulo reordering $P|Q \equiv Q|P$, too. So far, the parent-child relation is maintained only by name so that problems arise due to ambiguities if there are two ambients with the same name within a process.

Example 2.3 (Ambiguities in the net). The process term $m[P|m[Q]]$ corresponds to

This allows for several interpretations:

The last tree is the correct one but the representation allows for all of them.

The ambiguity becomes fatal as soon as capabilities are executed on unintended subtrees leading then to actually unreachable configurations. We will hence later use unique names $\mathcal{A} = \{a_i \mid i = 1, \ldots, n\}$ for all ambients. These newly assigned names are not in any relation to the original ones. Thus, we need to make sure that each capability knows "its" ambients.

Even with unique ambient names, yet another problem remains: Identical leaf process terms, so called twins, under one ambient hurt the one-safeness.

Example 2.4 (Multiple tokens in the presence of twins). We depict the situation for a double occurence of the leaf process term $P = \pi n.Q$ under a:

Fig. 2.1 The translation so far allows for multiple tokens.

We introduce unique identifiers $\mathbb{T} = \{T_s \mid i = 1, \ldots, n\}$, so called twigs, which we put instead of the leaf below its parent ambient. The relation to the actual leaf term P is maintained via places $T_s \cong P$:

Example 2.5 (Dealing with twins without and with twigs). With twigs, the situation from Figure 2.4 translates to

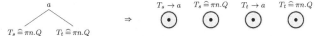

Fig. 2.2 Representing twigs in the net.

Although the introduction of twigs is a rather simple step, we will not incorporate them in our introductory constructions that simply transport the idea. They create a blow-up on every transition which may hide the central idea behind formalisms. The final construction presented in Section 3.2.2 will of course provide all features.

To separate the different groups of places with different functions we will use a colour encoding for the rest of this work. The colours are added step-by step and later summarised in Figure 3.1.

2.2 Translating Capability Actions into Petri Net Transitions

The MA calculus is a tree rewriting system since a change in the process state, i.e. the performance of a step according to the transition relation $\rightsquigarrow$ or the congruence $\equiv$, is a transition from one tree into another one.

Example 2.6 (Tree transition). Let $k \notin fn(P_2)$. We can then apply the scope extrusion:

The MA calculus solely provides actions with a local impact. All three capabilities only affect adjacent levels in the tree but behave quite differently on any other account. Our first rough translation of these actions will visualise which further information we should encode in our net in order to exclude behaviour impossible in MA. We will refine the construction by including twigs and the sophisticated name management. Restrictions are removed from the tree by the introduction of unique restricted link names $\mathcal{R} = \{r_i \mid i = 1, \ldots n\}$. Even though they are not yet introduced the reader may already assume a restriction-free tree. The call and some other operations are straight forward so that we will only depict them in Section 3.2.2 when we present the final translation for each MA construct.

We will now shortly summarise the capabilities' tree transitions. For the rest of this section we fix some naming conventions: Each process incarnation is contained in an ambient[1] which we call o. It is important to keep in mind that the process variables P, Q, and R used in MA's transition relation represent arbitrary process terms including those with an ambient or a parallel composition at the top level. However, in the case of $open\,m$ it will be important to highlight that such a process can be a parallel composition. We will do so by using Q_1 to Q_n instead of Q.

2.2.1 The Capability Action $in\,m$

The action $n[in\,m.P|Q]|m[R] \rightsquigarrow m[n[P|Q]|R]$ corresponds to:

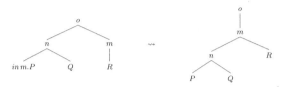

Fig. 2.3 $o[n[in\,m.P|Q]|m[R]] \rightsquigarrow o[m[n[P|Q]|R]]$

We make the parent n of $in\,m.P$ a child of its former sibling m. We neither depict Q nor R nor any further children of o in our net fragment since they do not interfere with the transition. In order to avoid n jumping through the tree we need to verify that they are siblings: We assumed that o is n's parent and thus need to check that it is also m's parent via a test on $m \to o$.

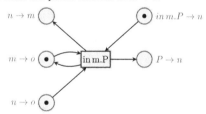

We depend on $in\,m.P$, o, and n for the transition. Thus, there is one such transition per $(o, n, in\,m.P)$-combination.

2.2.2 The Capability Action $out\,m$

The action $m[n[out\,m.P|Q]|R] \rightsquigarrow n[P|Q]|m[R]$ corresponds to:

Fig. 2.4 $o[m[n[out\,m.P|Q]|R]] \rightsquigarrow o[n[P|Q]|m[R]]$

---

[1] Remember that at least *root* is such an ambient.

The operation $out\,m$ is inverse to $in\,m$. The ambient n, formerly the parent of $out\,m.P$ and the child of ambient m, becomes m's sibling during the transition. Therefore, the transition has to know m's parent (which we assume to be o) to introduce n as its new child. This requires the test on $m \to o$ here.

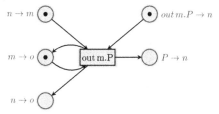

In comparison to an in transition, the $n \to m$ place is a token source while $n \to o$ now receives a token. Everything else is equal for both transitions (of course, now we consume the $out\,m$ prefix) and thus we again need one transition for each $(o, n, out\,m.P)$-combination.

2.2.3 The Capability Action open m

The action $open\,m.P \mid m[Q] \rightsquigarrow P \mid Q$ corresponds to:

Fig. 2.5 $o[open\,m.P \mid m[Q]] \rightsquigarrow o[P \mid Q]$

The ambient m is removed by its sibling $open\,m.P$. This requires *all* processes which were so far m's children to introduce themselves to m's and $open\,m.P$'s common parent o. Obviously, a new test on o is required but it can be realised with the change from $open\,m.P \to o$ to $P \to o$ which is anyway necessary.

Unfortunately, the Safe Petri net's structure so far is not able to decide *when* all subprocesses of m subscribed to o. We install complement places to overcome this short-coming. Now we may either inspect all place and complement place pairs in a predefined order or we can visit them concurrently. Since the latter approach requires an additional huge transition to unite the intermediate visits into an "all-ambients-considered" place – and since additional arguments will be necessary when arguing for the transitions' correctness – we will implement the first approach. Depending on the Petri net model checker at hand one may of course choose the concurrent approach instead.

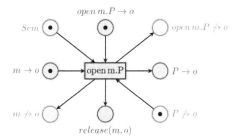

We use the semaphore to block other transitions which may influence the actual tree. This will prevent undesired races before we are able to restore a correct tree. After the actual $open\,m.P$ transition the tree is already degenerated into a forest since the connection $m \to o$ is erased. At first the second tree with root m possesses the children Q_1 to Q_n but during the chain's execution these children vanish. It doesn't make a difference whether an ambient or a leaf process is m's child so that we unite them in a set $M = \{P \mid P \text{ leaf term}\} \cup \{n \mid n \text{ name}\} \setminus \{m, o\}$ which we stepwisely process.

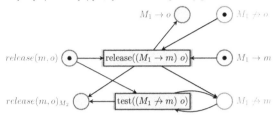

The chain is hard-coded via progress logging places $release(m, o)_{M_*}$ where $release(m, o)_{M_*}$ is consumed for the $(*+1)$-th transition and $release(m, o)_{M_{*+1}}$ is fed by it. We can unify the depicted first steps with all intermediate steps by a slight modification: Rather than $release(m, o)$ the open transition should fill $release(m, o)_{M_1}$.

The process chain provides the same two transition for each ambient or leaf process term M_* under m. In the case of a token on the complement place, nothing has to be done and the token is simply passed to the logger for the next step. However, if the token is on any place $M \to m$ we have to remove this connection and replace it by $M \to o$ before allowing the next transition to take over. The last transition re-installs the semaphore:

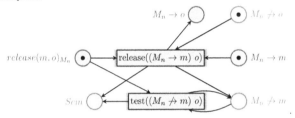

Finally, we are done and can be happy that only two ambients were involved. In fact, the release-chain only depends on the (m, o)-combination while the original open-transition depends on the $(o, open\, m.P)$-combination.

2.2.4 The Semaphore's Necessity

The usage of a semaphore on all transitions that modify the tree avoids races. We illustrate a race condition induced by the parallel execution of out and open on a child and its parent ambient in the example below.

Example 2.7 (Possible race without semaphore). We consider the process $o'[open\, o.S \mid o[m[n[out\, m.P \mid Q] \mid R]]]$. The initial open transition fires and its subsequent $release(o, o')$ sequence waits to be processed in parallel to the out m operation:

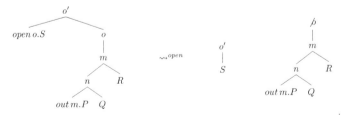

The ambient o should now vanish and all its children (here only m) should move under o'. If we now assume that the release chain starts its execution and the ambient n is tested ($\checkmark$) before out is fired, but

m is not, the token on $n \not\rightarrow o$ is seen and allows the test chain to proceed. Now *out* fires, thus n is hung under o. The release step on m correctly puts m below o' but the already tested n remains:

Since the n to o relation was already considered it won't be tested again so that n remains under the actually removed o and we run into an inconsistent system state. The new second root o should actually have vanished and n should be another child of o'. Instead, n's connection to the main tree is lost.

The strict use of the semaphore prevents such unpleasant behaviour. We now turn our attention to guaranteeing the uniqueness of names.

2.3 Managing Names in the Petri Net

As we pointed out in Example 2.3 the relation by name causes ambiguous trees since several ambients may carry the same name. We now use the ambient name set $\mathcal{A}$ which our Petri net will use instead of the original name. In order to react to the right capabilities the connection to that name is still maintained. We remove the restrictions from the tree by assigning a unique name from the new set of restricted link names $\mathcal{R}$. Their management requires new commands which we incorporate in the MA process equations via a preprocessing. We derive transitions to manage both link and ambient names.

Names and their respective positions store the information in the MA processes. The proof of Turing-completeness for the MA calculus [CG98, p. 149f] encodes the tape into a chain of nested ambients. The ambient's name corresponds to the current symbol on the dedicated tape position.

Example 2.8 (Ambient hierarchy encoding a word).

Fig. 2.6 Examplary word encoding: The word "hello" becomes "hell".

Hence, the saving of name and position information in each ambient is the heart of the information storage in the MA calculus. Capability operations and the addition of new ambients via ambient spawning $(n[P])$ manipulate such information.

2.3.1 Distinguishing Link from Ambient Names

Actually, a name m accomplishes two completely different tasks: It stores information in the ambient tree $(m[\ldots])$ via its name and position but it also maintains the connection between the ambients called m and the capability operations $(in\,m,\ out\,m$ and $open\,m)$.

We want to separate these concerns in our construction. Hence, we distinguish **link names** $(\mathcal{L})$, which maintain the connection between capabilities and the actual instance in the tree, and the globally unique instance names which we call **ambient names** $(\mathcal{A})$ and which form the tree. We demand $\mathcal{A} \cap \mathcal{L} = \emptyset$.

Example 2.9 (Distinguishing Link from Ambient Names).

Fig. 2.7 Distinguishing link from ambient names: Link name m and ambient name m.

Link names $\mathcal{L}$ unify all ambients in a scope and represent them in capabilities and process calls. We will enforce link names to be unique, too, so that we can manage their relation to the ambients $(a \mapsto l)$ by name and remove the restrictions from the tree. The incorporated ambients of one link name should not be affected by any other link name, nor should any ambient without a corresponding link name exist. Hence, the link names will induce a partition of the ambients into scopes.

Example 2.10 (A   capability's   scope). In   the   process $\nu m.(open\,m.P \,|\, m[Q_1] \,|\, m[Q_2])$ $|\,\nu m.(open\,m.P \,|\, m[R_1] \,|\, m[R_2])$ each *open* m-capability may only affect the two m-ambients in its restriction's scope. We assign the link names l_1 and l_2:

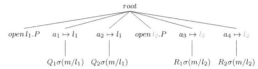

Fig. 2.8 Different scopes replaced by different names.

The omission of restrictions keeps the tree flat. Because of NC only locally restricted names may carry the same name. This makes a distinction between public link names $\mathcal{P}$ and restricted link names $\mathcal{R}$ appropriate. We have $\mathcal{L} = \mathcal{P} \cup \mathcal{R}$.

In summary, link and ambient names are globally unique but link names may occur several times within a process incarnation. They are only present at the leaf level, while the ambient names only occur above this level in the inner tree and at most once there.

2.3.2 Assigning a Restricted Link Name

We assign a new restricted link name $r \in \mathcal{R}$ whenever we process a leaf $\nu n.P$: The net non-deterministically chooses a currently unused name $r \in \mathcal{R}$ and substitutes n by r in the whole term P. Since n's scope can only be intermitted by a new νn which is not allowed within the same process equation due to NC we can substitute n by r on the whole leaf $(\nu n.P \rightsquigarrow P\sigma(n/r))$ without introducing a new restriction. It is necessary to rename the n-ambients as well: this propagates the information on which name r to link. Our substitution also replaces occurrences in process calls and thus makes sure that the name is passed on to subsequent equations.

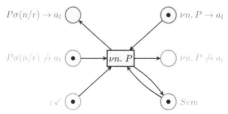

The token on $r\checkmark$ guarantees that r is currently unused. The transition occupies the name and performs $\nu n.P \rightsquigarrow P\sigma(n/r)$. The inner ambient hierarchy is not touched.

2.3.3 Assigning an Ambient Name

When processing an ambient spawn $l[P]$ we choose an arbitrary unused name $a_i \in \mathcal{A}$ ($a_i\checkmark$) and replace the link name $l \in \mathcal{L}$ by a_i, while not changing P at all. Note that this is no substitution on P but just a very local renaming in one position. We store the knowledge that a_i reacts to l-capabilities on the place $a_i \mapsto l$.

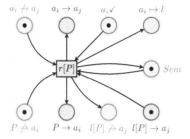

This transition is more complex than the link version since it must also integrate a_i into the ambient tree.

2.3.4 Releasing an Ambient Name

An ambient hierarchy remains even if there is no process running in it any more. This makes the release of an ambient name fairly easy, since the only situation to do so is when processing an *open* capability. There are only minor changes necessary to adapt the *open* procedure presented in Section 2.2.3. We now use the name l and write *open l* to indicate that we work on a link name.

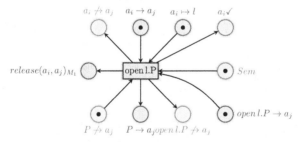

Due to the separation of link and ambient names we now need to check via a place $a_i \mapsto l$ that a_i reacts on l capabilities, namely on *open l*. We mark a_i as unused via $a_i\checkmark$ and erase a_i from the ambient hierarchy by the $release(a_i, a_j)$ procedure. This procedure remains unchanged in comparison to v2.2.3 and is hence not repeated here.

2.3.5 Releasing a Restricted Link Name

The releasing of a restricted link name is only possible if it is completely unused in the process incarnation P. In the marking representing this incarnation it should neither appear in a leaf process term nor have any ambient linked to it. A marking with a name r which is unused but not marked as unused ($r\checkmark$) corresponds to an MA process term $\nu r.P$ where r does not occur in P. In this analogy our release performs the congruence transformation to P that removes the unnecessary restriction.

We must start by verifying that the name is forgotten among all leaves since a leaf carrying a spawn could easily introduce a new link occurence in the ambient tree while an *open* command could remove one: As long as there are leaves using a name r there the information on its use in the tree is volatile.

2.3.5.1 Incorporating the Necessary Information — the Preprocessing

Whether or not a name is forgotten at the leaf level can best be monitored via the name's spread among the Petri net leaves. A name r's spread $s(r)$ is the number of Petri net leaves which currently use it. Although the spread's behaviour is totally dynamic the positions at which this value changes are already visible in the process equations. Thus, we can do a preprocessing on the original process equations with the original names. We mark the relevant positions on a name n with the commands $used(n)$ and $unused(n)$, respectively. These new commands allow the net to log the appropriate changes to a name's spread.

We determine the relevant positions by examining the right-hand side of each defining equation as well as the initial term. At first, only the leaf which carried the restriction νn can know the name n and thus later the chosen instance. Since there is no name passing mechanism like there is in the π calculus the leaf cannot spread its knowledge to other leaves arbitrarily. The name's spread can only increase if the leaf splits itself into two leaves. This can either happen due to a parallel composition or due to a replication. If after a parallel composition $P|Q$ both leaves use the name n we should increase $s(n)$ by 1.

Example 2.11 (Spread increase with parallel compositions). Both process terms following the parallel composition use n so that its spread increases as soon as this parallel composition is no longer prefixed.

Fig. 2.9 Counting leaves using n: n's spread changes from 1 to 2.

We can check for each parallel composition $P|Q$ in each defining equation (and in I) whether P and Q both continue to use a name n which was used before the parallel composition. If they do, we put the command $used(n)$ before the parallel composition. One could argue that this increases the spread too early, before the parallel composition is actually processed, but since we are only interested in the question whether the spread is above 0 or not this can cause no harm.

However, if we put the $used(n)$ command say in front of Q we could reach wrong conclusions: Imagine $s(n) = 1$, that is the leaf carrying $P|Q$ is the only leaf knowing n. If we now freed P for execution it could easily reach and execute its $unused(n)$ out of which the net would conclude $s(n) = 0$ although Q still knows n but did not tell the net yet.

The dealing with the replication $!P$ is similar to that for the parallel composition: we must put a used command right behind the replication sign ! for each name occurring in P. But since a name occurring in a replication term can never become unused our spread count is useless there. We only keep it to exclude the wrong conclusion of a spread of 0 which may otherwise arise just like it may in the parallel composition's case.

The $unused$ commands are put behind each last occurrence of a name on the right-hand side of a process equation. Due to $minPara$ in Definition 1.5 this last occurrence is always either a capability or a spawn. Thus, we check behind each capability πn and spawn $n[Q]$ whether n is used in the following process term Q. If it is not used we put the $unused(n)$ command before Q.

2.3.5.2 Forgotten Among All Leaves? — Maintaining a Name's Spread

The new commands are executed during runtime and thus performed on the instance name r. As soon as a spread declines to 0 we immediately know that the respective name is forgotten among all leaves $(r\sqrt{_{leaves}})$. The one-safeness requires us to use one place $s(r) = i$ per possible spread value i. Whenever we process a restriction $\nu n.P$ we initialise the spread of the chosen name r with 1.

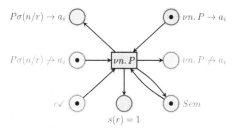

The substitution $P\sigma(n/r)$ and subsequent calls also instantiate the corresponding *used* and *unused* commands with r.

Each $used(r)$ action increases r's current spread $s(r) = i$ by 1:

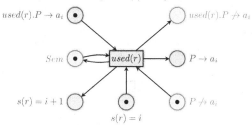

The $unused(r)$ action behaves similarly, but reduces the spread by moving the token from $s(r) = i$ onto $s(r) = i - 1$. In every case but the lowest option with $s(r) = 1$ we simply have:

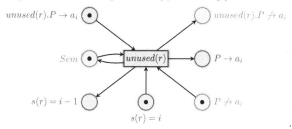

If r's spread is $s(r) = 1$ before the $unused(r)$ execution, the name is now forgotten among all leaves. Instead of $s(r) = 1$ we remove the count completely and mark $r\checkmark_{leaves}$.

Commands can be set for a name r freshly restricted in this term as well as for a formal parameter x inherited from some former process term. The latter may cause problems if the name instantiating x is public. We can easily deal with these problems by an additional transition for each public name $p \in \mathcal{P}$ which simply consumes the command:

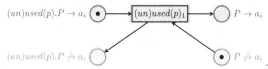

Another way to address this problem is to exclude public names from parameter lists as we will discuss in Section 4.1.4.

2.3.5.3 Forgotten in the Ambient Tree

As soon as the instance r is forgotten among all leaves we also need to make sure that no ambient is linked onto r. Here the static relationship between an ambient and its link name plays an important role: During an ambient's whole life time it is bound to one link name. Only by opening it becomes free again and can then be assigned to a new link name l during a spawn. However, we know that this new name isn't our name r since r is forgotten among all leaves and therefore cannot exist in a spawn.

Thus, we only have to implement a simple test chain where we protocol for each ambient name $a \in \mathcal{A}$ that it is not linked to r. As we discussed before it does not matter *when* we test the ambients as long as the name r is forgotten among all leaves. This makes the consuming of the semaphore unnecessary for the whole procedure which we again implement sequentially.

Each of the chain's transitions takes a place $unused(r)_{a_*}$ as input[2]. This place encodes that all ambients up to a_* have already been inspected and none of them was linked onto r. The ambient a_* is next. The possible situations are:

- $a_* \mapsto r$: If a_* is linked onto r we may not proceed but are trapped. Since no r capabilities exist any more this ambient and its link to r will never be removed. Thus, r will never become unused.
- $a_* \mapsto l_r \neq r$: If a_* is linked onto a name different to r we can immediately proceed to a_{*+1}.
- $a_*\checkmark$: The ambient name a_* is currently unused. It cannot become linked to r since no spawn on r exists. Thus, we can immediately proceed to a_{*+1}.

The corresponding transition set is:

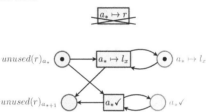

The transition for the link name l_x stands subsidiarily for all $\mathcal{L} \setminus \{r\}$ transitions. We reflect the blocking by no transition in the case that a_* is linked onto r. If the chain passes all ambients successfully the last transition marks the name r as unused ($r\checkmark$).

2.4 Guaranteeing Finiteness

So far, we were not worried about the finiteness of the Petri net. With our design decision to maintain the tree by using distinct identifiers for each ambient and twig we are forced to limit their respective numbers. We introduce a breadth bound b which gives a bound for $\mathbb{T}$ and an additional bound d to limit the overall number of ambients and thus $\mathcal{A}$. A bound for $\mathcal{R}$ can be constructed out of them.

Definition 2.12 (b,d-bounded process). An MA **process term** is called b,d-bounded if its number of ambients is at most d and the overall number of parallel compositions is at most $b - 1$, that is there are at most b leaf processes. An MA **process** is called b,d-bounded if each reachable congruence class contains at least one b,d-bounded instance.

Conceptually, the bound d is a depth bound for the ambient tree and thus for the process since it constraints the nesting depth of ambients. A depth bound on MA processes was also necessary in [RVMS12] where they derived decidability of coverability by a translation into ν-MSR. This logic incorporates a restriction ν which makes it convenient for the translation but hard for the checking – only a non-primitive recursive coverability checking procedure exists and reachability is in general undecidable. However, the restriction operator allows them to enforce uniqueness by different scopes rather than different names so that their result is independent of any breadth bound. It is unknown whether pure MA reachability is decidable if we only require a depth bound. But since it is known to be undecidable for MA's ancestor π ([MG09, p. 15])

---

[2] To avoid the distinction between the chain's first and intermediate transitions, we mark $unused(r)_{a_1}$ instead of $r\checkmark_{leaves}$ in $unused(r)$.

where depth is the number of names a "leaf" process knows we expect it to require high complexity if at all possible for MA. Our breadth restriction allows for an only PSPACE-complete decidability procedure which is as low as one can usually get in verification.

The breadth and depth bounds are in general not computable since this would allow us to decide how much space a Turing machine uses. Recall that MA can simulate arbitrary Turing machines (Argument in Section 2.3 subsuming the proof in [CG98, p. 149f]). Rather than restricting the process to be b, d-bounded we could therefore set artificial bounds to generate a finite net. Even if the process itself was unbounded it might possess interesting runs – e.g. counter-examples – which respect the artificial bounds. Section 4.1.2 will provide the necessary extensions and a small example. The reader who finds it more convenient may already check that all translation schemes in principle extend to unbounded processes, too. Only the simulation may block if we require more names or twigs than we have: We can process a parallel composition or a replication only if a new twig is available for the new leaf. This requires a management of unused twigs T_s via places $T_s\checkmark$ which is similiar to the ambient name management.

Apart from the breadth and depth bound there are some size parameters which depend on the respective MA process (D, I) where each $D_i \in D$ has a parameter vector $\vec{x}_i$. We call the maximal number of parameters in a defining equation $\kappa = max_{D_i \in D}(|\vec{x}_i|)$. We have the number of public names p and the number of process equations $d_D = |D|$.

The maximal number c of restrictions a leaf process term may spawn is crucial for the possible calls: Only public, freshly restricted names and passed restricted names are possible parameters. We must compare all possible threads through each process equation in order to determine c. Since a parallel composition splits one leaf into two we have to consider both resulting subprocess terms in combination with the part before the split. Thus, we multiply out each parallel composition: $A.(P|Q)$ is transformed to $A.P$ and $A.Q$. Of course, the results are not equivalent to the process term before since instead of one shared name we now receive two independent names n for each restriction νn in the prefix A. If we apply the transformation to each process equation including I we receive a number of threads Th_i with $i = 1, \ldots, m$. The maximal number c of new restrictions is simply the maximal number of restrictions in one of these threads $c = max(\#\nu(Th_i) \,|\, i = 1, \ldots, m)$. It is obvious that all of the process parameters are bound by the process's size n.

Chapter 3
Translating MA Processes into Safe Petri Nets — Complete Construction

To maintain a finite set of link names we must realise when such a name becomes unused, that is the binding ν is obsolete. The positions are statically determinable and we mark them with additional calculus terms. Since this exceeds the MA syntax we define a refined MA calculus rMA and prove its bisimiliarity with MA in Section 3.1.

We then define the one-bounded Petri net that reflects an arbitrary rMA term and show how to translate rMA into this so-called MA-PN in Section 3.2. Already this net is finite if and only if the MA term is bounded Finally, we establish a second bisimulation in Section 3.3, this time linking rMA and MA-PN so that we can conclude the bisimiliarity of MA and MA-PN by the transitivity of bisimulations. The construction is not yet polynomial since the possible name combinations in calls are exponential. This flaw is easily removed by a substitution net [MKH12] but we defer this addition to the appendix in order to avoid clutter.

3.1 From MA to rMA

The introduction of the *used* and *unused* commands exceeds the MA calculus's means. We therefore define the **refined MA calculus**, shortly called rMA calculus, which is capable of expressing the additional commands. We give and analyse the preprocessing algorithm which bridges the gap between the two formalisms. The proof that rMA introduces no new behaviour is done by establishing a bisimulation. It is our first step towards a bisimulation between MA and our Petri nets.

3.1.1 The Refined MA Calculus

Since rMA is a rather simple extension of MA we will only give new definitions where necessary and otherwise expect the given MA definition to extend to rMA as well.

Definition 3.1 (Syntax). P is an rMA process term if it is built according to the following rules: $P ::= 0 \mid \pi.P \mid n[P] \mid \tau.P \mid !P \mid \nu n.P \mid P|Q \mid K(\vec{a})$, where $\pi = \{in\,n,\ out\,n,\ open\,n\}$ and $\tau = \{used(n), unused(n)\}$ for a name n.

This is essentially the same definition as Definition 1.2, only the new commands are added. We give τn the same binding priority as πn, otherwise adopting the priorities given for the MA calculus. Additionally, we need to adapt the transition relation in order to deal with the new actions.

Definition 3.2 (Transition relation for rMA). The rMA transition relation is that of the MA calculus with the additional rules:

> **use:** $used(n).P \rightsquigarrow P$
> **unuse:** $unused(n).P \rightsquigarrow P$

Thus, the new commands are simple silent actions where the prefix is consumed but no modification on the tree is necessary. They play no role in rMA's semantics and do not influence the system behaviour. However, we know that the Petri net will take a quite different view on them.

We adapt the structural congruence given in Definition 1.3 accordingly by the addition of $P \equiv Q \Rightarrow \tau.P \equiv \tau.Q$ with $\tau = \{used(n),\ unused(n)\}$.

3.1.2 Preprocessing MA

The bridge towards rMA is the preprocessing algorithm for the introduction of *used* and *unused* commands to an MA process $\mathcal{P} = (D, I)$. We consider the initial term I as the right-hand side of a parameterless equation $D_j \in D$ so that we then simply deal with all defining equations. The set $rn(D_i)$ consists of those names which are freshly restricted in D_i.

We need a predicate $occur(n, P)$ which tests syntactically wether the name n occurs in the term P. It can be implemented linearly in $length(P)$ which is always in $\mathcal{O}(length(D_i))$. The actual algorithm $pre(\mathcal{P})$ is performed independently for each $D_i \in D$ by the following replacement:

> **for each** $\pi n.P$:
>   **if not** $occur(n, P)$ **then set** $\pi n.unused(n).P$
> **for each** $n[P]$:
>   **if not** $occur(n, P)$ **then set** $n[unused(n).P]$
> **for each** $P|Q$:
>   **for each** $n \in \vec{x}_i \cup rn(D_i)$:
>   **if** $occur(n, P)$ **and** $occur(n, Q)$ **then set** $used(n).(P|Q)$
> **for each** $!P$:
>   **for each** $n \in \vec{x}_i \cup rn(D_i)$:
>   **if** $occur(n, P)$ **then set** $used(n).P$

Since capability and spawn address a single name we can set at most one *unused* command behind each one of them. On the contrary, it may be necessary to put several *used* commands before a parallel composition or a replication – one for each name which is spread to P and Q or used in P.

The algorithm can be implemented by one pass through the process term which determines the respective positions to be checked. Of course, neither the number of capabilities and spawns nor of parallel compositions and replications may exceed $length(D_i)$. The check behind a capability and spawn only requires one execution of $occur$ while each parallel composition may require up to $|\vec{x}_i \cup rn(D_i)| \cdot 2$ many executions which is twice as much as the replication requires. Although dominating the capabilities' and spawns' time demand those are still in $\mathcal{O}(length(D_i))$. Thus, even in the worst case where the equation mostly consists of parallel compositions we are still in $\mathcal{O}(length(D_i))^2$ for its analysis. This guarantees that our preprocessing for all equations may be performed in $\mathcal{O}(n^3)$ for $n = size(\mathcal{P})$.

3.1.3 Bisimulation between MA and rMA

MA and rMA calculus enjoy the prototype of weak bismiulation since their only difference lies in the silent actions which rMA has while MA doesn't have them. As already implied by Lemma 1.11 any process term derived out of a term P by adding silent actions to P is bisimilar to it.

Lemma 3.3. *Let P an MA process. The relation $\simeq_\mathcal{P} = (P, pre(P))$ linking an MA process and the rMA process derived by preprocessing it is a bisimulation.*

Proof. The rMA process $pre(P)$ is an enrichment of P by silent $used$ and $unused$ actions. No reordering or replacement of the MA process's actions happens. Thus, we can establish a bisimulation between the two processes by Lemma 1.11. □

We can define a b,d-bounded rMA process in analogy to Definition 2.12. Since we will establish a Petri net translation only for b,d-bounded MA processes it is desirable to know that the bisimulation $\simeq_\mathcal{P}$ between MA and rMA processes retains the bounds.

Lemma 3.4. *Let P a b,d-bounded MA process. The rMA process $pre(P)$ is also b,d-bounded.*

Proof. Neither a $used$ nor an $unused$ command can make a process deeper since they are only located at the leaf level. Since $used$ is always placed behind a capability it cannot extend the depth, either.

To show that $unused$ cannot enlarge the breadth, we analyse the possible breadth contributions of $P|Q$. If at least one process term doesn't equal 0, $P|Q$ contributes at least with 1 to the breadth. Thus, the breadth of $used(n).(P|Q)$ is at most as large as the breadth of $P|Q$. Only if $P|Q = 0|0$, the parallel composition doesn't contribute to the breadth. However, in this case pre doesn't introduce any $used$ action, either. Analogously, we do not put any $used$ command if $!P = !0$. □

3.2 The Resulting MA-Petri Nets MA-PN

The Petri nets we introduce are constructed out of a b,d-bounded (r)MA process. This is why we call them MA-Petri nets, shortly MA-PN. Each net will need an rMA process P as construction parameter. We show how to use this process to derive the sets $\mathcal{R}$, $\mathcal{P}$, $\mathcal{L}$, $\mathcal{A}$, $\mathbb{T}$, and $\mathbb{B}$ which are then used to compile the places in Section 3.2.1.2. Purely based on them Section 3.2.2 depicts and analyses all transitions.

Definition 3.5 (MA-PN). Let $\mathbb{P}$ a b,d-bounded rMA process. The MA-PN($\mathbb{P}$) is the Petri net $(P(\mathbb{P}), T(\mathbb{P}), F(\mathbb{P}), M_0(\mathbb{P}))$ with $P(\mathbb{P})$ as defined in Section 3.2.1.2, $M_0(\mathbb{P})$ as defined in Section 3.2.1.4, and $F(\mathbb{P})$ and $T(\mathbb{P})$ following the building schemes of Section 3.2.2.

3.2.1 Places and Markings

We first construct the rather simple sets $\mathcal{R}$, $\mathcal{P}$, $\mathcal{L}$, $\mathcal{A}$, and $\mathbb{T}$ out of the process's parameters and the breadth and depth bound before we turn our attention to the leaf level in Section 3.2.1.1. All sets are then used to determine the places $P(\mathbb{P})$ in Section 3.2.1.2. Afterwards we propose a graphical notation for a net marking in Section 3.2.1.3 which facilitates the definition of the initial marking in Section 3.2.1.4.

Definition 3.6 (MA-PN sets). Let $\mathbb{P} = (D, I)$ a b, d-bounded rMA process and p the number of public names, c the maximal number of restrictions in a thread, and κ the maximal number of call parameters. We define its associated MA-PN sets $\mathcal{R} = \{r_1, \ldots, r_{b \cdot (\kappa + c) + d}\}$, $\mathcal{P} = fn(\mathbb{P})$, $\mathcal{L} = \mathcal{P} \cup \mathcal{R}$, $\mathcal{A} = \{a_1, \ldots, a_d\}$, and $\mathbb{T} = \{T_1, \ldots, T_b\}$.

3.2.1.1 All Possible Leaves – Buds

A last prerequisite for the compilation of the Petri net places is a precise notion of the leaf terms. So far we considered them as those terms which are leafs in the (r)MA tree. This would match the concept of derivatives which were introduced in [Mey09] for the π-calculus and extended to the MA calculus by [RVMS12, p. 27]. However, we take a lazy approach to the net's behaviour and also allow for unprocessed parallel compositions and ambient spawners at the beginning of a leaf process.

Thus, the set of all possible leaves – conveniently called buds – can be defined in the following way:

Definition 3.7 (MA-PN set of buds). Let $\mathbb{P} = (D, I)$ a b, d-bounded rMA process and $D = \{D_1, \ldots, D_n\}$, $\vec{x}_i$ the list of formal parameters for the defining equation D_i, and $\vec{a}$ the actual parameters. Based on the associated MA-PN set $\mathcal{R}$ we define a last associated set $\mathbb{B} := b(I)$ where

$$
\begin{aligned}
b(0) &:= \{0\} & b(D_i(\vec{a})) &:= \{D_i(\vec{a})\} \cup b(D_i \sigma(\vec{x}_i / \vec{a})) \\
b(\pi.P) &:= \{\pi.P\} \cup b(P) & b(n[P]) &:= \{n[P]\} \cup b(P) \\
b(![P]) &:= \{![P]\} \cup b(P) & b(\nu n.P) &:= \{\nu n.P\} \cup \bigcup (b(P \sigma(n/r) \mid r \in \mathcal{R}) \\
b(P \mid Q) &:= \{P \mid Q\} \cup b(P) \cup b(Q) & b(\tau.P) &:= \{\tau.P\} \cup b(P)
\end{aligned}
$$

When removing a restriction νn we replace the rMA name n promptly by all possible restricted link names $r \in \mathcal{R}$. Each call happens with the actual parameters only. This can require at most $|\mathcal{L}|^{\kappa_i}$ many initial settings for D_i. With each restriction producing $|\mathcal{R}|$ many new ways to proceed there are up to $|\mathcal{L}|^{\kappa_i} \cdot |\mathcal{R}|^{c_i} \cdot |D_i|$ many buds per D_i which is not polynomial since we only know that $c_i \in \mathcal{O}(n)$ and $\kappa_i \in \mathcal{O}(n)$. The name on which a spawn is later executed will always be a link name.

The use of a substitution net as introduced in [MKH12] will make our construction polynomial but also quite overwhelming. We therefore work with the exponential $\mathbb{B}$ but present the necessary modifications in Appendix B. For now we have $|\mathbb{B}| \in \mathcal{O}(|\mathcal{L}|^{\kappa_i} \cdot |\mathcal{R}|^{c_i} \cdot |D_i| \cdot d_D) \in \mathcal{O}(|\mathcal{L}|^{\kappa_i + c_i} \cdot |D_i| \cdot d_D) \in \mathcal{O}(|\mathcal{L}|^n \cdot n^2)$.

3.2.1.2 All MA-PN Places

We are now prepared to determine the set of places $P(\mathbb{P})$. We shortly recapitulate each associated MA-PN set's purpose and determine its size.

$\mathbb{T}$: Twigs are unique separators between leaves and inner tree. They were introduced in 2.1 to guarantee one-safeness by separating twins. We defined $\mathbb{T} = \{T_1, \ldots, T_b\}$, thus $|\mathbb{T}| = b$.

$\mathcal{A}$: The ambient names form the inner tree. They were introduced in Section 2.3.1. We defined $\mathcal{A} = \{a_1, \ldots, a_d\}$ and now add $\mathcal{A}' = \mathcal{A} \cup \{root\}$ so that we have $|\mathcal{A}| = d$ and $|\mathcal{A}'| \in \mathcal{O}(d)$.

$\mathcal{R}$: Restricted link names guarantee uniqueness of restricted names. They were introduced in Section 2.3.1. We set $\mathcal{R} = \{r_1, \ldots, r_{b \cdot (\kappa + c) + d}\}$ and have $|\mathcal{R}| \in \mathcal{O}(b \cdot (c + \kappa) + d)$.

$\mathcal{P}$: Public names are globally unique. In MA-PN they only occur at the leaf level. They were also introduced in Section 2.3.1. We set $\mathcal{P} = fn(\mathbb{P})$ and thus conclude $|\mathcal{P}| = p$.

$\mathcal{L}$: Link names occur in leaves only and represent several ambient names. They were introduced in Section 2.3.1. We defined $\mathcal{L} = \mathcal{P} \cup \mathcal{R}$, so that $|\mathcal{L}| \in \mathcal{O}(p + |\mathcal{R}|)$.

$\mathbb{B}$: The buds are all possible leaves introduced in Section 3.2.1.1. We have $|\mathbb{B}| \in \mathcal{O}(|\mathcal{L}|^n \cdot n^2)$.

Additionally we need to determine how many places we must reserve at most as possible spread values. The actual spread cannot exceed our breadth bound b since this is the limit on the number of leaves. However, our approach to place $used(n)$ before the parallel composition allows the spread to increase further. It may never exceed $2 \cdot b$, though, so that we use the spread values $I = \{1, \ldots, 2 \cdot b\}$. The set M abbreviates $\mathcal{A} \cup \mathbb{T}$. We now depict all places and highlight their respective function.

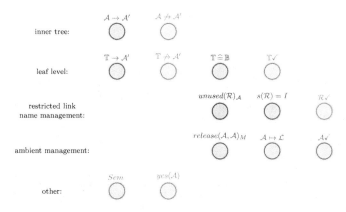

Fig. 3.1 The Petri net places.

One just multiplies the involved sets' sizes to determine the respective number of places. Apart from $\mathbb{T} \cong \mathbb{B}$, for which we have $|\mathbb{T}| \cdot |\mathbb{B}|$ and thus exponentially many places, all numbers are polynomial in the process size and the bounds.

3.2.1.3 MA-PN Trees for Stable Markings

Often, we are only interested in the tree behind an MA-PN marking. It is sufficient to visualise the transformation a particular transition performs and thus allows us to reason about the transitions' correctness. We will build our bisimulation between rMA processes and MA-PN on the insight that the respective MA-PN transitions perform the depicted MA-PN tree transition.

The tree can already be determined from the places $\mathcal{A} \to \mathcal{A}'$, $\mathbb{T} \to \mathcal{A}'$, $\mathbb{T} \cong \mathbb{B}$, $\mathcal{A} \mapsto \mathcal{L}$, and Sem. The semaphore is necessary to distinguish markings encoding a tree from intermediate markings in the *open* chain. We call a marking **stable** if it possesses the semaphore. Otherwise it is called unstable and may relate to a forest as we saw in Section 2.2.3.

The MA-PN Tree

We depict the ambient tree with the chosen ambient names $a_i \in \mathcal{A}$, and the additional note onto which link name $l \in \mathcal{L}$ each ambient reacts. The twigs are shown as leaves with their assigned bud notated just behind. Thus, an MA-PN tree may look like this:

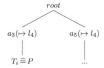

Fig. 3.2 An MA-PN tree for the process $l_4[P] \mid l_4[\dots]$.

It might sometimes be helpful to use a calculus notation rather than the tree. We will therefore simply treat the tree's entries as if they were an rMA tree's respective names. For the above example we would have $root[a_3(\mapsto l_4)[T_i \cong P]\mid a_5(\mapsto l_4)[\dots]]$ as short notation. We will devote Section 3.3.1 to proving that the MA-PN transitions between stable markings maintain a uniquely determinable tree.

3.2.1.4 Initialising the Net

We initialise the net by assigning the initial process I to the twig T_1 which is then the $root$'s only child:

All other ambient and twig relations are marked as not present via the complement places. The corresponding twigs are marked as unused just as all the ambient and link names are. We place a token on the semaphore. The Petri net will use its ambient spawning, restriction processing, and parallel composition splitting transitions to establish an ambient hierarchy out of the initial term.

3.2.2 Transitions

We distinguish MA-PN transitions which correspond to rMA actions or parts of them from other transitions which allow a transformation within an rMA equivalence class. When we depict the tree transition we highlight this distinction by the use of $\rightsquigarrow_{MA-PN}$ and $\equiv_{MA-PN}$, respectively.

We introduce transitions for each possible bud prefix. Since the processing of a parallel composition or the removal of an unnecessary 0 leaf are new, we present them with the necessary care and explanation. Most other transitions are only recapitulated and the reader is referred back towards the introducing section for further discussion. Some tree transitions are included as to allow for a quick check of the correspondence between marking and tree. Our proofs will later rely on this insight.

We will not include the replication in our studies here since it generates what its name promises – unboundedly many leaves and thus unbounded breadth. Thus, a b, d-bounded MA process cannot contain an executable replication. Section 4.1.2 will deal with the replication again but until then we use a fragment without it.

The subsection is divided into two parts where the first part shows all transition (chains) which form MA-PN actions and the second part gives all equivalence transformations. We use distinct identifiers out of the associated MA-PN sets, namely $T_s, T_t \in \mathbb{T}$, $a_i, a_j, a_k \in \mathcal{A}$, $l \in \mathcal{L}$, $r \in \mathcal{R}$, and $p \in \mathcal{P}$. This will allow us to distinguish distinct elements of the same set within one transition. In the case of the test chain we iterate over all ambient names so that we additionally use a_d to indicate the chain's last element. The transition $a_* \mapsto \mathcal{L} \setminus \{r\}$ stands for the set of similar transitions for each element in $\mathcal{L} \setminus \{r\}$ per fixed restricted link name r and varying but per set fixed ambient a_*.

3.2.2.1 Transitions for rMA Actions

We will only consider transitions and transition chains that each lead from one stable marking to the next. Single transitions of a chain are grouped together so that the whole mimicking of an rMA action is presented coherently.

Moving Branches: The Capability Action $in\,l$

We (re-)implement the idea presented in Section 2.2.1. Due to the extensive changes we now need the test on the semaphore, complement places, twigs, and a distinction between the ambient a_i in the tree and the corresponding link name l instead of the former MA name m.

Of course, o's instance a_k may have more children than the n instance a_j and the l instance a_i but they are not touched by this transition. We use additional link names l_n and l_o instead of the MA names n and o to clarify the distinction but miantain the connection to our former construction. We thus translate the rMA action $l_o[l_n[in\,l.P|(*)]|l[(**)]] \rightsquigarrow l_o[l[l_n[P|(*)]|(**)]]$ which is

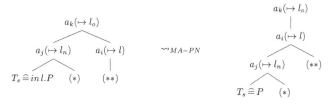

under the assumption that we use the ambient name a_i for the depicted instance of l, a_k as l_o instance and a_j as l_n instance.

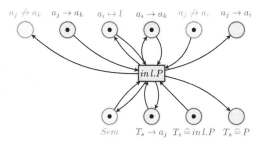

The former change from $in\,m.P \to n$ to $P \to n$ is now done in the twig T_s by a change from $T_s \mathrel{\widehat{=}} in\,l.P$ to $T_s \mathrel{\widehat{=}} P$. T_s is no longer the child of n – or l_n – but of its instance which is here called a_j. We need the test on $T_s \to a_j$ and on $a_i \to a_k$ together with the knowledge $a_j \to a_k$ to be sure that the $in\,l$ command is called under a sibling of a_i.

We implement one transition per ambient name a_i, a_j, and a_k, bud $in\,l.P$ which also determines P, and the involved link name l. Thus, there are $\mathcal{O}(|\mathcal{A}| \cdot |\mathcal{A}| \cdot |\mathcal{A}| \cdot |\mathbb{B}| \cdot |\mathbb{T}|)$ many transitions.

Moving Branches: The Capability Action *out l*

Since the *out* command is inverse to *in* we can reuse the *in l* transition with the slight change already proposed in 2.2.2 when processing the ambient hierarchy: We take a token from $a_j \to a_i$ and put one onto $a_j \to a_k$ which is just opposite to the taking and giving for *in l*.

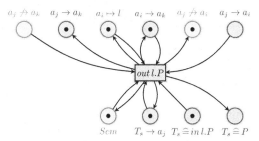

In analogy to the processing of *in* the necessary number of transitions is $\mathcal{O}(|\mathcal{A}| \cdot |\mathcal{A}| \cdot |\mathcal{A}| \cdot |\mathbb{B}| \cdot |\mathbb{T}|)$.

Releasing an Ambient when Processing *open l*

Each processing of an *open l* command destroys one ambient a_i linked onto l. All its children have to assign themselves to a_i's former parent ambient which we assume to be a_j. This is done via the $release(a_i, a_j)$ procedure. Thus, this is the first rMA action that cannot be performed in one Petri net transition. The *open* transition is equivalent to that introduced in Section 2.3.4, only twigs are included:

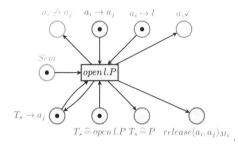

The transition depends on the involved ambients a_i and a_j, the associated twig T_s, and the process $in\,l.P$ which also determines l. M_1 is fixed by an assumed order on the set M. Thus, there are overall $\mathcal{O}(|\mathcal{A}| \cdot |\mathcal{A}| \cdot |\mathbb{B}| \cdot |\mathbb{T}|)$ many transitions.

The blocking chain of transitions iterates over all possible children of the destroyed ambient a_i to relink them onto a_i's parent a_j. These possible children are all ambients but a_i and a_j, and – now rather than all leaves – all twigs which we unite under $M = (\mathcal{A} \setminus \{a_i, a_j\}) \cup \mathbb{T}$. All intermediate transition pairs jump from $release(a_i, a_j)_{M_*}$ to $release(a_i, a_j)_{M_{*+1}}$:

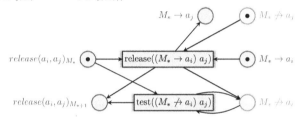

and the last transition pair sets Sem rather than the non-existing M_{m+1} for $|M| = m = b + (c+\kappa)\cdot b + d - 2$:

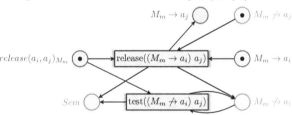

We need $|M| \in \mathcal{O}(|\mathcal{A}| + |\mathbb{T}|)$ many such transitions for each (a_i, a_j)-combination which makes overall $\mathcal{O}((|\mathcal{A}| + |\mathbb{T}|)\cdot |\mathcal{A}|^2) \in \mathcal{O}(|\mathcal{A}|^3)$ many transitions.

Calling an Equation $K(\vec{a})$

The call of an equation $K(\vec{a})$ also only affects the leaf level. There the call term $K(\vec{a})$ is replaced by its corresponding equation K with the parameter substitution $\sigma(\vec{x}/\vec{a})$.

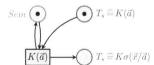

We need one transition per bud $K(\vec{a})$ and twig T_s, thus $\mathcal{O}(|\mathbb{B}| \cdot |\mathbb{T}|)$ many transitions.

Processing $used(r)$

The $used(r)$ command is a silent action for rMA which hence neither affects the inner tree nor does more to the leaves than consuming the $used(r)$ prefix. In the MA-PN each $used(r)$ action is "loud" and increases r's current spread $s(r) = i$ by 1:

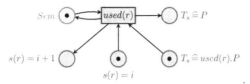

There is one transition per current spread $s(r) = i$ with $i \in \{1, \ldots, 2 \cdot b - 1\}$. Each of these transitions occurs per twig T_s and bud $used(r).P$ which also determines r. This makes overall $\mathcal{O}(|\mathbb{T}| \cdot |\mathbb{B}| \cdot (2 \cdot b))$ many transitions.

Additionally, we need the dummy transitions for public names $p \in \mathcal{P}$.

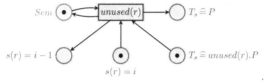

There are $\mathcal{O}(|\mathbb{T}| \cdot |\mathbb{B}|)$ many such silent transitions.

Processing $unused(r)$

The $unused(r)$ action behaves similarly, but reduces the spread by moving the token from $s(r) = i$ onto $s(r) = i - 1$. We distinguish $s(r) = i$ with $i \in \{2, \ldots, 2 \cdot b\}$ from $s(r) = 1$ as current spread. The transition for higher spreads is:

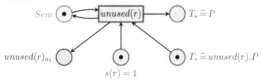

The lowest case requires a minor change: Rather than setting $s(r) = 0$ we set $unused(r)_{a_1}$ to initialise the test chain over all ambients.

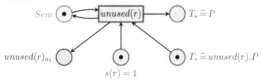

The complexity argumentation presented for $used(r)$ also holds for the $unused(r)$ case. The $s(r) = 1$ version is in $\mathcal{O}(|\mathbb{T}| \cdot |\mathbb{B}|)$ which is dominated by $\mathcal{O}(|\mathbb{T}| \cdot |\mathbb{B}| \cdot (2 \cdot b))$ which holds for the cases with higher spread. Thus, we have $\mathcal{O}(|\mathbb{T}| \cdot |\mathbb{B}| \cdot (2 \cdot b))$ $unused(r)$ transitions.

Additionally, we need the silent transitions for public names $p \in \mathcal{P}$:

$$T_s \cong unused(p).P \quad \boxed{unused(p)} \quad T_s \cong P$$

There are $\mathcal{O}(|\mathbb{T}| \cdot |\mathbb{B}|)$ many such transitions which are also dominated by $\mathcal{O}(|\mathbb{T}| \cdot |\mathbb{B}| \cdot (2 \cdot b))$.

3.2.2.2 Transitions for Equivalence Transformations

We now turn to all those transitions and transition chains that lead from one marking of an equivalence class to another one. These transitions can be very important – as in the case of a twig removal that allows a formerly hindered parallel composition to execute – but do not contribute to any MA-PN action. We only implemented the equivalence transformations that lead to markings that are better in our sense, that is, have less unused but still marked restricted link names, 0-carrying twigs, unexecuted parallel compositions, and therelike.

Occupying a New Twig: Parallel Compositions $P|Q$

As discussed in Section 3.2.1.1 we take a lazy approach to the process behaviour by allowing parallel composition $P|Q$ as one leaf. Still, further steps like the processing of the first operator in P or Q can only be done after the removal of the composition so that we have to separate P and Q into two subprocesses which should each be assigned to an own twig. In the terms of rMA nothing is changed, the rMA process term $l[P|Q]$ remains. However, we can highlight the difference on the MA-PN tree:

Fig. 3.3 Occupying a second twig.

Of course, we can reuse the former twig T_s so that only one unused twig T_t is necessary. As discussed in Section 2.4 the presence of an unoccupied twig T is indicated by the place $l\sqrt{}$ in the net. Out of the currently unused twigs one is chosen at random. We assume ambient a_i representing l as parent of the twig T_s carrying the parallel composition $P|Q$ and show the transition splitting it by occupying T_t.

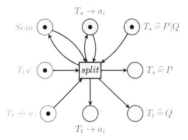

We claim the unused twig T_t for our transition by consuming the token on $T_t\sqrt{}$. Also, we test that a_i is T_s's parent and thus know that we have to assign T_t to a_i as well. We need one transition per $(P|Q, a_i, T_s, T_t)$-combination. Hence, there are $\mathcal{O}\left(|\mathbb{B}| \cdot |\mathcal{A}| \cdot |\mathbb{T}| \cdot |\mathbb{T}|\right)$ many *split*-transitions.

Removing Dead Twigs

We call a twig carrying 0 only a dead twig. We will implement the rMA congruence rules which allow one to cut such dead twigs under certain conditions. There is only one case in which such a twig should remain: Consider the case where the 0 leaf is the only leaf under an ambient chain. The chain contributes to the process's breadth which is maintained via the number of twigs. If we removed the twig we would allow the process to exceed its bound by assigning the twig to a new subprocess.

Hence, we need to distinguish several cases to react properly to the different situations the twig carrying the 0 leaf could be in:

1. *root* **as parent:** If rather than an ambient chain only *root* is the parent of twig T_s we may remove the 0 leaf and its associated twig without further worries. In the worst case we implement $0 \equiv \varepsilon$.
2. $\mathcal{A}$ **as parent, T_s only child:** If an ambient a_i is T_s's parent and there is no sibling of T_s we may neither touch leaf nor twig because the 0 leaf may later be processed if one of the other situations is present then.
3. $\mathcal{A}$ **as parent, T_s has siblings:** If an ambient a_i is T_s's parent and we found at least one sibling we may remove 0 leaf and twig.

Thus, there are only two situations to take action which for us means to define transitions. We cannot implement a transition to simply remove the 0 leaf if we have to keep the twig T_s (situation 2) since this would destroy the information that T_s carries a 0 leaf and would hence make it impossible to apply a 0 transition if one of the situations 1 and 3 became true.

Situation 1 – *root* as parent: The transition for the first case transforms $root[0]$ to $root[]$. If 0 possesses siblings R we implement $0|R \equiv R$, if 0 is the only process left, we implement $0 \equiv \varepsilon$. In the terms of our Petri net tree representation that is:

$$
\begin{array}{ccc}
root & & root \\
\diagup \diagdown & \equiv_{MA-PN} & | \\
T_s \hat{=} 0 \quad \dots & & \dots
\end{array}
$$

The Petri net transition mimics this behaviour. Additionally, T_s is marked as free for further use and can now be requested by another leaf process term.

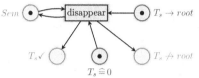

This transition only depends on the choice for T_s. Thus, there are $\mathcal{O}(b)$ root based disappear transitions.

Situation 3 – $\mathcal{A}$ as parent, T_s has siblings: We implement $R|0 \equiv R$ in case 3. There is an ambient $a_i \in \mathcal{A}$ with one child T_s and at least one other child. This second child can either be another twig T_t with an arbitrary leaf process P underneath:

$$
\begin{array}{ccc}
a_i(\mapsto l) & & a_i(\mapsto l) \\
\diagup \diagdown & \equiv_{MA-PN} & | \\
T_s \hat{=} 0 \quad T_t \hat{=} P & & T_t \hat{=} P
\end{array}
$$

or the second child can be another ambient $a_j \in \mathcal{A}$:

$$
\begin{array}{ccc}
a_i(\mapsto l) & & a_i(\mapsto l) \\
\diagup \diagdown & \equiv_{MA-PN} & | \\
T_s \hat{=} 0 \quad a_j(\mapsto \dots) & & a_j(\mapsto \dots) \\
| & & | \\
\dots & & \dots
\end{array}
$$

The difference between these two situations is only technical. If one of the situations is present the net may immediately cut one twig with a 0 leaf. Hence, we test wether all conditions except for the existence of a twig T_s with a 0 leaf hold under the ambient a_i and store the result in a place $yes(a_i)$. This information is used in a second transition which cuts one dead twig under a_i if one is present.

The two test transitions do some kind of local snapshot on a_i's children and use $yes(a_i)$ to announce the situation. To maintain the consistency between net and snapshot the transition takes the semaphore, thus allowing for no modification in the tree. Also, this makes sure that at most one token is put on $yes(a_i)$, even if both conditions are fulfilled.

However, this transition is not triggered by some leaf process but is a guess on the (unlikely) situation that a_i possesses a twig carrying 0 underneath. In the case of a wrong guess the whole system blocks. This does no harm to the semantics or correctness of the net but may cause serious problems in an implementation. It is easily overcome by the addition of a *wrong guess* transition which destroys the information on $yes(a_i)$ and re-installs the semaphore.

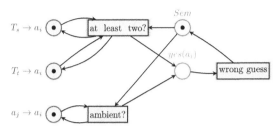

There is no enforcement on the involved twigs but we simply test wether there are at least two twigs under a_i so that one of them could carry a 0 and be removed. Of course, there may be more twigs present but so far we are only interested in wether there are enough twigs to remove one dead twig. This allows us to produce one *at least two?* transition per twig pair which is $|\mathbb{T}| \cdot (|\mathbb{T}| - 1) \in \mathcal{O}(|\mathbb{T}|^2)$ of these transitions per name a_i, thus overall $\mathcal{O}(|\mathbb{T}|^2 \cdot |\mathcal{A}|))$ many transitions. Additionally, there is one *ambient?* transition per name apart from a_i so that there are $|\mathcal{A}| - 1$ per name and overall $\mathcal{O}(|\mathcal{A}| \cdot |\mathcal{A}|)$ *ambient?* transitions. The *wrong guess* transition exists once per $yes(a_i)$ place and thus $\mathcal{O}(|\mathcal{A}|)$ many times.

Instead of *wrong guess* a second transition which removes the dead twig may fire. It is independent from the technical details tested before but uses the right to cut one dead twig under a_i which is granted by the token on $yes(a_i)$. The transition deletes the twig and its 0 leaf and re-installs the semaphore, thus allowing other subprocesses to go on. The twig T_s is marked as unused again.

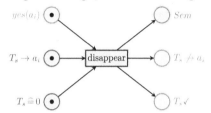

This *disappear* transition is only dependent on the twig T_s and the parent ambient a_i so that we need $\mathcal{O}(|\mathbb{T}| \cdot |\mathcal{A}|)$ many such transitions.

Using a New Link Name by Processing a Restriction νn

As discussed in Section 2.3 the restriction νn only affects the leaf level, the inner tree is not touched. The idea already shown in that section remains, but due to the introduction of twigs we do not care for a parent ambient any more. Hence, we only depend on the twig T_s and the chosen instance $r \in \mathcal{R}$:

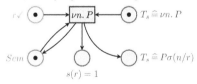

We need one transition per restricted link name r, twig T_s, and bud $\nu n.P$, since the second involved bud $P\sigma(n/r)$ is determined completely by $\nu n.P$ and r. This makes overall $\mathcal{O}(|\mathcal{R}| \cdot |\mathcal{A}| \cdot |\mathbb{T}| \cdot |\mathbb{B}|)$ many transitions.

Untriggered Test on Restricted Link Names

The testing of a restricted name r is not triggered by a leaf command but may be done as soon as the leaves report that the name is forgotten among them by a token on the chain's initiator $unused(r)_{a_1}$. We now test that it is also forgotten in the ambient hierarchy. Iterating over the elements a_* of $\mathcal{A}$ the chain presented in Section 2.3.5.3 remains:

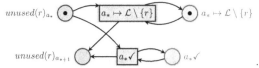

There is one $a_* \mapsto l$ transition for each link name $l \in \mathcal{L}$ but r and one additional transition for the case that a_* possesses no link but is unused. Together this makes $\mathcal{O}(|\mathcal{L}|)$ transitions per ambient name a_* and fixed link name r. The sequence's last transition marks r as unused ($r\checkmark$):

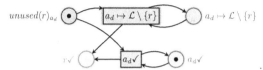

Iterating over all possible ambient names $a_* \in \mathcal{A}$ per restricted link name $r \in \mathcal{R}$ makes a total number of $\mathcal{O}(|\mathcal{A}| \cdot |\mathcal{R}| \cdot |\mathcal{L}|)$ transitions since each transition set consists of $|\mathcal{L}|$ transitions.

Integrating a New Ambient into the Tree via $l[P]$

We refine the transition from Section 2.3.3 by incorporating twigs, link names, and the semaphore. When processing a twig T_s carrying an ambient spawner $l[P]$ we have to move a freshly chosen l instance a_i past T_s into the tree. Therefore, we have to replace T_s's relation to its parent a_j by one to a_i and announce a_i in turn as a_j's child.

Fig. 3.4 Processing a spawn on the link name l in an MA-PN tree.

As discussed in Section 2.3 the name l in $l[P]$ is always a link name. We need to claim an unused ambient name $a_i \in \mathcal{A}$ which we link on l ($a_i \mapsto l$) and then move into the tree.

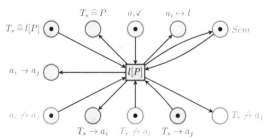

There is one transition per parent ambient a_j, twig T_s, bud $l[P]$, and newly occupied ambient a_i. Thus, we need $\mathcal{O}(|\mathcal{A}| \cdot |\mathcal{A}| \cdot |\mathbb{T}| \cdot |\mathbb{B}|)$ many transitions.

3.3 From rMA to MA-PN

MA-PN markings should conform to trees for we set them up to mimic rMA processes which are known to have a tree structure. We first prove that each MA-PN transition between any two markings doesn't destroy formerly holding uniqueness constraints. The uniqueness of an ambient's link and parent, a twig's parent, and bud together with cycle-freeness of the parent relation guarantees that the resulting structure is a forest. We can further prove that if a stable marking corresponded to a tree with root *root* any other stable marking reachable by MA-PN transitions also conforms to such a tree.

In Section 3.3.2.1 this result allows us to define a function *rest* which translates a stable MA-PN marking into a tree that is then transformed into an rMA process term. We refine the construction further to recover the original process term before we turn our attention to the formal establishment of rMA's and MA-PN's connection via processed markings. These markings can simulate all actions possible in the corresponding rMA process term. They can be constructed using equivalence transitions only as we show in Section 3.3.2.4. Thus our bisimulation in Section 3.3.3 between rMA and MA-PN relies on them.

For the rest of this section and in all following sections we will only consider MA-PN markings which are reachable in at least one MA-PN. So we let M a reachable MA-PN marking, i.e. it is produced out of an initial MA-PN marking $root[T_1 \cong I]$. This excludes pathological cases, e.g. situations where $a\checkmark$ and $a \mapsto r$ are both marked.

3.3.1 Stable MA-PN Markings Maintain a Tree Structure

For the rest of this subsection we will use the MA-PN's places' names as predicates which are true in a marking iff the respective place holds a token. We will use an arbitrary reachable MA-PN marking M as a model for our formulas. S is a further restriction of M which is also stable.

3.3.1.1 Uniqueness Invariants

We inductively prove some uniqueness invariants which together guarantee that each stable marking is a graph with out-degree ≤ 1 for each node. We first show that the mapping to a link name $l \in \mathcal{L}$ is unique for each ambient a. If the ambient name is currently unused, it is not linked to any link name.

Lemma 3.8 (Uniqueness of each ambient's link). *Let $a \in \mathcal{A}$ an ambient name.*

$$M \models [(\exists! l \in \mathcal{L}. a \mapsto l) \wedge \neg a\checkmark] \vee [(\forall l \in \mathcal{L}. \neg a \mapsto l) \wedge a\checkmark]$$

Proof. In the initial marking each ambient is marked as unused and no link is installed. This conforms to the second case described above.

Now we should check wether all transitions maintain the invariant. We assume that it holds in the transition's pre-state. Of course we can restrict our search to those transitions which change an ambient's link or usage. They are:

- Capability *open* in 3.2.2.1: The *open l* transition releases an ambient named a_i. It removes the $a_i \mapsto l$ link while installing a token on case 2, thus transferring case 1 into case 2.
- $l[P]$ in 3.2.2.2: The ambient spawner $l[P]$ performs the opposite step by occupying a new ambient name a_i, thus removing the token on $a_i\checkmark$ and installing one on $a_i \mapsto l$. This transfers case 2 into case 1. □

Each ambient name $a \in \mathcal{A}$ has at most one parent:

Lemma 3.9 (Uniqueness of an ambient's parent). *Let $a \in \mathcal{A}$ an ambient name.*

$$M \models \quad [\neg a\checkmark \wedge (\exists! l \in \mathcal{A}'. a \to l \wedge (\forall l' \in \mathcal{A}'. l' \neq l \Rightarrow a \not\to l'))]$$
$$\vee [a\checkmark \wedge (\forall l \in \mathcal{A}'. a \not\to l)]$$

Proof. The initial marking conforms to the second case described above for all ambients. We have to check wether all transitions maintain the invariant.

Of course we can restrict our search to those transitions which change ambient relations and assume that the invariant holds in the transition's pre-state. They are:

- Capability *in* in 3.2.2.1: The *in l* transition can only fire if case 1 is present on an ambient name a_j: $a_j \to a_k$ holds before the transition and is then replaced by its complement $a_j \not\to a_k$. According to the invariant either a new parent for a_j should be installed or a_j should be marked as free. The transition remains in case 1 by putting a token on $a_j \to a_i$ and removing its complement token.

- Capability *out* in 3.2.2.1: The *out l* transition also goes from case 1 to case 1 now moving the token from $a_j \to a_i$ to $a_j \to a_k$.
- Capability *open* in 3.2.2.1: The *open l* transition requires case 1 on an ambient name a_i by the token on $a_i \to a_k$ and performs the change to case 2 by marking the name as free and replacing $a_i \to a_k$ by its complement place. The succeeding *release* transitions perform a change within case 2 since they change the ambient's link from a_i to a_k.
- $l[P]$ in 3.2.2.2: The ambient spawner $l[P]$ performs the step from case 2 to case 1. It occupies a so far unused name a_i and moves it under a_k by removing the token on $a_i \not\to a_k$ and putting it on $a_i \to a_k$. $\square$

This lemma proves that exactly the used names have a parent and that this parent is unique. It could also be written as

$$M \models \quad [\neg a \checkmark \Leftrightarrow (\exists! \, l \in \mathcal{A}'. \, a \to l \wedge (\forall l' \in \mathcal{A}'. \, l' \neq l \Rightarrow a \not\to l'))] \wedge [a \checkmark \Leftrightarrow (\forall l \in \mathcal{A}'. \, a \not\to l)].$$

We can prove the same property for the lowest tree level: Each twig $T \in \mathbb{T}$ has a unique parent ambient or is currently unused.

Lemma 3.10 (Uniqueness of a twig's parent). *Let $T \in \mathbb{T}$ a twig.*

$$M \models \quad [\neg T \checkmark \wedge (\exists! \, l \in \mathcal{A}'. \, T \to l \wedge (\forall l' \in \mathcal{A}'. \, l' \neq l \Rightarrow T \not\to l'))] \vee [T \checkmark \wedge (\forall l \in \mathcal{A}'. \, T \not\to l)]$$

Proof. The initial marking represents case 1 for the twig T_1 since it is assigned to *root*, and represents the second case for all other twigs. We have to check wether all transitions maintain the property.

Of course we can restrict our search to those transitions which change a twig's ambient relation and assume that the invariant holds in the transition's pre-state. They are:

- $P|Q$ in 3.2.2.2: The parallel composition occupies a new twig T_t, thus requiring case 2 on T_t and transforming it into case 1. The relation on T_s is not touched.
- Twig removal in 3.2.2.2: The *disappear* transitions takes the opposite approach by removing the $T_s \to a_i$ relation and installing its complement. Additionally, T_s is marked as unused so that we indeed go from case 1 to case 2.
- Release in 3.2.2.1: During the *release* chain, each twig T assigned to the freshly opened ambient a_i is hung under a_j. This is a transition within case 1, since $T \to a_i$ is replaced by its complement and $T \not\to a_j$ is replaced by $T \to a_j$.
- $l[P]$ in 3.2.2.2: The ambient spawner transition $l[P]$ moves the token from $T_s \to a_j$ to $T_s \to a_i$ with the necessary complement operations. It is another transition within case 1. $\square$

Each twig T is assigned at most one bud. If there is no bud assigned to T it is marked as unused.

Lemma 3.11 (Uniqueness of the twig's bud). *Let $T \in \mathbb{T}$ a twig.*

$$M \models [(\exists! \, b \in \mathbb{B}. \, T \,\hat{=}\, b) \wedge \neg T \checkmark] \vee [(\forall b \in \mathbb{B}. \, \neg T \,\hat{=}\, b) \wedge T \checkmark]$$

Proof. The initial marking on the relevant places conforms to the second case described above. We have to check wether all transitions maintain the invariant.

Unfortunately, nearly every transition changes at least one twig's bud so that we group the relevant transitions instead of discussing them one by one. We again follow the inductive proof scheme by assuming that the invariant holds in the transition's pre-state. The involved transitions are:

- $P|Q$ in 3.2.2.2: The *split* transition requires case 2 on T_t. It removes the tokens on $T_t \checkmark$ and $T_t \not\to a_i$ and installs a new one on $T_t \to a_j$ so that we produce a case 1 situation on T_t. The parallel composition 3.2.2.2 changes T_s's bud from $P|Q$ to P maintaining the uniqueness and staying within case 1.
- Twig removal in 3.2.2.2: The two *disappear* transitions remove a $T_s \,\hat{=}\, 0$ token and mark the twig T_s as unused. Thus, they move from case 1 to case 2.
- Capabilities *in* in 3.2.2.1, *out* in 3.2.2.1, and *open* in 3.2.2.1, $l[P]$ in 3.2.2.2, $\nu n.P$ in 3.2.2.2, $K(\vec{a})$ in 3.2.2.1, *used* in 3.2.2.1, and *unused* in 3.2.2.1: All of these transitions perform a prefix removal on T_s's bud which is a transformation within case 1. $\square$

3.3.1.2 Each Stable Marking Represents a Tree

So far we know that our represented structure is a graph with out-degree ≤ 1 for every node. In oder to prove it a tree (or forest) we have to show that no cycles exist.

Lemma 3.12 (Cycle-freeness). *Each reachable MA-PN marking represents cycle-free parent-child-relations among all its ambients and twigs.*

Proof. Of course, the initial marking is cycle-free, it is a very simple tree. In order to maintain cycle-freeness it is enough to guarantee that each new relation maintains the so far used direction, that is no ambient is ever made child of one of its children. We can concentrate on the ambients completely since the twigs are anyway kept below them and without relations between each other.

Transitions changing ambient relations are:

- Capabilities: The transitions *out* and *open* change an ambient's parent relation from parent to grandparent, *in* moves an ambient below its sibling.
- $l[P]$: The spawn introduces a so far unused ambient to the tree. This introduction happens below every other ambient.

Thus, no ambient is ever linked onto one of its children. □

By combining the lemmata we already know that each marking represents a forest.

Lemma 3.13 (Forest). *Each reachable MA-PN marking M represents a forest.*

Proof. The combination of the four Lemmata 3.9, 3.10, 3.11, and 3.12 proves that each MA-PN marking conforms to an (MA-PN) forest. □

To get the stronger result that each stable marking conforms to one tree with root *root* we investigate all sequences between stable markings.

Lemma 3.14 (Tree). *Each reachable stable MA-PN marking S represents a tree with root root.*

Proof. It is obvious that the condition holds for the initial marking $root[T_1 \cong I]$ itself. Now we will prove that any transition (sequence) from one stable marking S_1 to the next one S_2 maintains this invariant. We only care for transitions which influence the parent-child relations between ambients and twigs.

One can easily verify that only one transition sequence with intermediate unstable markings can be executed at a time since each first step consumes the semaphore and each later step requires the one before. The untriggered *test* sequence shown in Section 3.2.2.2 is independent of the semaphore. Thus, it may be executed between stable markings or interleaved with an arbitrary blocking chain. However, its transitions do not influence the tree and can be ignored. The following transitions remain:

- $P|Q$ in 3.2.2.2: The newly installed ambient relation $T_t \to a_i$ may not introduce a distinct tree since $T_* \to a_i$ already holds and thus a_i is part of the one tree S_1 depicts.
- Twig removal in 3.2.2.2: Both twig cutters only remove a twig but introduce no new relation.
- $l[P]$ in 3.2.2.2: The new ambient is integrated into the existing tree.
- Capabilities *in* in 3.2.2.1 and *out* in 3.2.2.1: Both transitions perform a local change in the tree. No new relations are introduced.
- Capability *open* in 3.2.2.1: The transition *open l.P* cuts the relation between a_i and a_j so that the subtree with root a_i becomes a distinct tree, a_i is already marked as unused. The *release* chain moves all subtrees from under a_i back under a_j. Since a_i is already marked as unused this removes the newly created tree completely.

Thus, each stable marking represents a tree with root *root*. □

3.3.2 Connection between rMA and MA-PN

We use this section to make the connection between rMA and MA-PN precise. While an MA-PN needs an rMA process as construction parameter the opposite direction is not so clear. Therefore we first define a function to restore an rMA process out of a stable MA-PN marking. The former result of Lemma 3.14 that each stable marking represents a tree guarantees that we indeed define a function. We highlight the restored process term's connection to the original rMA process and define an equivalence on markings based on this connection in Section 3.3.2.2.

Not every marking in an MA-PN equivalence class can execute all actions the corresponding rMA process can execute, thus this equivalence is no congruence. Processed markings are introduced as exit points of the equivalence classes: a processed marking can execute exactly the same actions as its original rMA process term. In Section 3.3.2.4 we show that the MA-PN transitions can transform each stable marking into an equivalent processed marking so that we can limit our bisimulation in Section 3.3.3 to processed markings.

3.3.2.1 Restoring rMA Process Terms

We will use the respective trees to relate rMA process terms and MA-PN markings. With a fixed order on link names and buds we can establish a function $rest(M)$ which produces an rMA process term P out of an MA-PN marking M by dropping unnecessary information.

To transform an MA-PN tree into a corresponding rMA tree, only few modifications are necessary. We can drop the twigs and the concrete ambient names and place the buds and link names in the hierarchy instead.

Example 3.15 (From MA-PN tree to rMA tree). We drop the information introduced in MA-PN to guarantee uniqueness:

The introduced *root* remains so that we still have a tree rather than a forest.

Of course, this will most likely lead to link names appearing several times within the tree. However, the situation is still clear since the tree is unique (up to reordering of the branches). It may still contain "lazy" leaves, that is leaves which start with an unprocessed restriction, ambient or parallel composition. But these peculiarities disappear automatically when we transform the tree into a process term.

We must then also choose an order on each node's respective children. As discussed in Section 2.1 we can take any choice because the resulting processes are congruent to each other by the parallel composition's commutativity $P|Q \equiv Q|P$. We may discard the *root* now.

3.3.2.2 Recovering the Original Process Term

The process $rest(M)$ is already a correct rMA process. However, all processed restrictions are missing since they were replaced by unique restricted link names $r \in \mathcal{R}$. Thus, this process term may contain many more public names than the original rMA process term out of which we constructed the MA-PN marking M. Luckily, we can simply bind the whole process term $rest(M)$ under MA-PN's set $\mathcal{R}$ to recover the original process term. Of course, some of the names $r \in \mathcal{R}$ may not be used in the process so that their binding is unnecessary. But since $\nu\mathcal{R}.P \equiv \nu\mathcal{R}'.P$ where $\mathcal{R}'$ only includes the restricted names used in P we do not have to deal with this. One can approximate $\mathcal{R}'$ by a look on the places $r\surd$ with $r \in \mathcal{R}$: at least these names are not used in the net.

Definition 3.16 (Associated rMA process). Let M a stable MA-PN marking with the set of restricted link names $\mathcal{R}$. Its associated rMA process term R is

$$R = \nu\mathcal{R}.rest(M)$$

where *rest* is the restoring function for a process term introduced above.

This unique correspondence from the marking's point of view is matched by a large number of markings for each process: The function $rest(M)$ abstracts the different possible choices for twig and ambient names away. Also, it hides wether some leaf contained unprocessed ambient spawns or parallel compositions. Only the mapping for the restricted names is specified.

Definition 3.17 (Associated markings). Let R a b,d-bounded rMA process term. Its associated MA-PN markings are all those stable markings M for which $R = \nu\mathcal{R}.rest(M)$ holds.

This definition separates markings which took a different choice on the restricted link names although we know that these choices can be exchanged by α conversion. Further aspects are the number of 0 leaf terms and other technical issues. We define an equivalence on markings to unite those which correspond to the same rMA congruence class.

Definition 3.18 (Equivalence on markings). We call two markings M and M' of an MA-PN with restricted names $\mathcal{R}$ equivalent if their associated rMA process terms are equivalent.

$$M \equiv_{MA-PN} M' \quad \text{iff} \quad \nu\mathcal{R}.rest(M) \equiv \nu\mathcal{R}.rest(M')$$

All markings in an equivalence class modulo $\equiv_{MA-PN}$ are exactly those markings which are in association to the same process term up to $\equiv$. Thus, the notion of association also extends to equivalence classes.

Since the equivalence on rMA process terms is a congruence, every representative of the same equivalence class can perform the same actions. This is guaranteed by the rules $P \rightsquigarrow Q \Rightarrow n[P] \rightsquigarrow n[Q]$, $P \rightsquigarrow Q \Rightarrow \nu n.P \rightsquigarrow \nu n.Q$, and $P \rightsquigarrow Q \Rightarrow P \,|\, R \rightsquigarrow Q \,|\, R$. This is different for MA-PN: Only leaf prefixes may be processed in an MA-PN marking but capabilities, restrictions, and parallel compositions can also form such a prefix. Thus, a covered capability, call or silent action cannot be executed even if the covering element is just a restriction. This leads to several markings in the same equivalence class which can only execute a subset of the actions their associated rMA process term can. We did not implement all necessary rules to move from an arbitrary marking M to all equivalent ones via MA-PN transitions. Instead we only implemented transitions which lead to a "better" marking, that is a marking which is able to perform more rMA actions. "Best" are the processed markings:

Definition 3.19 (Processed markings). We call a stable marking processed if

1. All its leaves are a call or 0 or start with a capability or a silent action.
2. Each restricted link name $r \in \mathcal{R}$ is either marked as unused or is indeed used.

This definition captures all those markings which can execute exactly the same actions as their associated rMA process since all leaves start with an rMA action. The second criterion guarantees some kind of normalisation on the restricted link names: there is no completely executable *test* chain in the middle of its execution.

3.3.2.3 Understanding Processed Markings: rMA's Restricted Normal Form

We present a normal form for rMA process terms which is in close correspondence to processed markings: If we recover the associated process term to a processed marking M it is always in restricted normal form (RNF). Roughly speaking, the RNF allows inner restrictions only if they are guarded by a capability or silent action. Exactly those restrictions are also present in a processed MA-PN marking.

Definition 3.20 (RNF). An rMA process term R is in restricted normal form (RNF) if

$$R ::= \nu n_1 \ldots \nu n_k.P$$

where $P ::= 0 \mid n[P] \mid P_1|P_2 \mid K(\vec{a}) \mid \pi.P' \mid \tau.P'$
and $P' ::= 0 \mid n[P'] \mid P_1'|P_2' \mid K(\vec{a}) \mid \pi.P' \mid \tau.P' \mid \nu n.P'$
where π denotes a capability and τ denotes a silent (un)use action.

One can easily verify that there is an equivalent process term in RNF for an arbitrary rMA process term.

Lemma 3.21 (Transformation into RNF for any rMA process). *For each rMA process term R there is an rMA process term R' in RNF for which $R \equiv R'$ holds.*

Proof. Any process term can be transformed into one in RNF by applying the following congruence rules:

1. $\nu n.(P \,|\, Q) \equiv (\nu n.P) \,|\, Q$ if n not free in Q
2. $\nu n.m[P] \equiv m[\nu n.P]$ if $n \neq m$
3. $\nu n.\nu m.P \equiv \nu m.\nu n.P$

Since we want to enlarge each quantifier's scope we apply the first two rules in the opposite direction to the way they are written here. If another restriction with the same name blocks the movement of one restriction e.g. $\nu n.n[\nu n.(open\, n.0)]$, the restriction wanting to go up renames itself by a name substitution:

$$\nu n.n[\nu n.(open\, n.0)] \equiv \nu n.n[\nu m.(open\, m.0)] \equiv \nu n.\nu m.(n[open\, m.0]) \qquad \square$$

In every RNF process term the restrictions form one long chain above the actual tree with its behaviour. Each restricted name is unique in the tree just like it is in an MA-PN marking. The net guarantees uniqueness by introducing so far unused names $r \in \mathcal{R}$. Afterwards it can drop the useless restrictions rather than moving them to the outside.

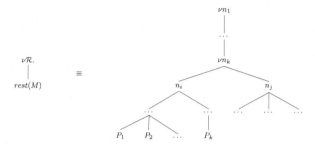

Fig. 3.5 Correspondence between a processed MA-PN marking M and the RNF.

3.3.2.4 Producing Processed Markings

We show that we can produce an equivalent processed marking out of each stable MA-PN marking using the MA-PN transitions. Therefore we first turn our attention to the second condition for a processed marking: A name should either really be used or marked as unused. We show that we can mark each unused name as unused and stay within the same equivalence class.

Lemma 3.22 (Release of restricted names). *Let M a stable MA-PN marking and $r \in \mathcal{R}$ forgotten among all leaves and not referenced as link by any ambient in the ambient tree. The forgotten r is either marked as unused or can immediately, that is without further consumption of the semaphore be marked as unused. The new marking is equivalent to the old one.*

Proof. If a name r is forgotten among all leaves, it was either never in use or all $used(r)$ and $unused(r)$ commands were executed: The preprocessing installs these commands and a forgetting implies their execution since they are not present on the leaves any more. In the former case r is marked as unused by the initial marking. Hence, we can turn our attention to the latter case.

The execution of the commands implies that the place $unused(r)_{a_1}$ was or is marked: The current marking can either represent this situation or some further step including $r\checkmark$ in the processing of the test chain presented in Section 3.2.2.2. This chain is the only way to change these particular markings concerned with r.

The chain is a simple test which does not change any part of the tree. It only moves a token from $unused(r)_{a_1}$ to $unused(r)_{a_d}$ and further onto $r\checkmark$ to protocol its progress in testing that no ambient is linked onto r. Thus, for any intermediate marking M' after the execution of some part of the chain it holds that $M \equiv_{MA-PN} M'$ since already $rest(M) = rest(M')$. After the whole execution r is indeed marked as unused. $\square$

This is also an important prerequisite for the reuse of a restricted link name which is necessary when we process a restriction. Additionally, we must show that our restricted link name set $\mathcal{R}$ was chosen huge enough, so that whenever our MA-PN marking requires a new restricted link name one is indeed unused (or can be marked as unused).

Remember that we assigned $b \cdot (c + \kappa) + d$ restricted link names where b and d are breadth and depth bound, c is the maximal number of new restrictions, and κ the maximal number of parameters. We first show that no MA-PN marking blocks more than this number of restricted names.

Lemma 3.23 (Blocking restricted names on leaves). *Let M an MA-PN marking. One leaf can block at most $c + \kappa$ restricted names.*

Proof. Each leaf can only contain – and thus use – $c + \kappa$ different restricted link names. This is the worst case assumption where κ different restricted names are passed as parameters and the c new restrictions are processed before the first *unused* command becomes the leaf prefix. Idealised, this is $P(\vec{x}) = \nu\vec{n}.\ldots Q(\vec{y})$ where the length of $\vec{x}$ and $\vec{y}$ is κ and $\vec{n}$ has length c. Of course, no further restrictions may be present in the omitted inner part[1] since the maximum c is already reached. Before the final call $Q(\vec{y})$ all necessary (which is here at least c) *unused* commands are processed so that at most κ used names may persist the call. □

Example 3.24 (Periodic name usage). We depict the number of names used in the process $P(\vec{a})$ where $P\llcorner\vec{x}\lrcorner = \nu n_1.\ldots\nu n_c.n_c[unused(n_c).open\,x_4.unused(x_4)\ldots Q(n_2, n_2, \ldots)]$. We assume that $\vec{a}$ consists of κ different restricted link names so that we have κ different known names right after the call of P.

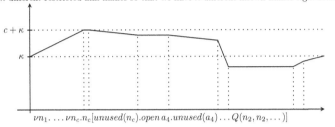

Since at least some parameters in the final call to Q are the same the number of known names is guaranteed to be below κ.

Over all leaves this makes at most $b \cdot (c + \kappa)$ different restricted names. If names occur among different leaves this keeps the number below this bound since such a name contributes to both leaves' bounds.

Lemma 3.25 (Blocking restricted names in the tree). *Let M an MA-PN marking. The ambient hierarchy can block at most d restricted link names.*

Proof. Each ambient name $a \in \mathcal{A}$ possesses a unique link $a \in \mathcal{L}$. With $|\mathcal{A}| = d$ at most d link names may be blocked by the ambient hierarchy. Only if all of these names are different restricted link names we reach the bound. □

Combining the lemmata we can determine $b \cdot (c + \kappa) + d = b \cdot (c + \kappa) + d$ as bound for $\mathcal{R}$.

Lemma 3.26 (Restricted link names suffice). *Let M a stable MA-PN marking. If M contains a leaf $T_s \hateq \nu n.P$ starting with a restriction, it either contains an unused name $r \in \mathcal{R}$ ($\cdot\sqrt{\ }$) or can transform itself into an equivalent marking M' in which a restricted name is marked as unused.*

Proof. The net possesses $b \cdot (c + \kappa) + d$ restricted link names. We assume the worst case proven in Lemma 3.25 so that indeed d restricted names are blocked by the ambient hierarchy. Each leaf but $\nu n.P$ may use at most $c + \kappa$ different restricted names by Lemma 3.23 so that the other leaves block at most $(b - 1) \cdot (c + \kappa)$ restricted names. Now T_s's leaf may still use up to κ restricted names which were supplied to it as call parameters. However, it cannot already use c new names since a restriction νn is still present in the leaf and thus less than c restrictions were so far processed. Thus, at least one restricted name is unknown among all leaves and does not appear as link in the tree. By Lemma 3.22 this name can be marked as unused immediately while maintaining the equivalence. □

We now show that the marking *after* the processing of such a restriction is also in the same equivalence class.

Lemma 3.27 (Equivalence when processing restrictions). *Let M a stable MA-PN marking. We assume that the transition $\nu n.P$ from 3.2.2.2 with the names used there is enabled. Let M' the marking after the execution of this one transition. $M \equiv_{MA-PN} M'$ holds and M' is stable as well.*

Proof. The transition only tests on the semaphore so that the stability is guaranteed. It performs a step

---

[1] We do not have to worry about parallel compositions in the omitted part since their processing will simply lead to one new twig T_t on which the same arguments hold.

where the upper dots hide the above ambient hierarchy A and the right dots encode arbitrary siblings denotable as process R. Thus, $rest(M_1) = rest(A)[\nu n.S|rest(R)] \rightsquigarrow rest(M_2) = rest(A)[S\sigma(n/r)|rest(R)]$.
We need to prove the equivalence of the associated rMA processes $P_1 = \nu\mathcal{R}.rest(M_1)$ and $P_2 = \nu\mathcal{R}.rest(M_2)$ since by Definition 3.18 this proves equivalence of the markings. We have $P_2 = \nu\mathcal{R}.rest(A)[S\sigma(n/r)|rest(R)] \equiv \nu\mathcal{R}^*.\nu r.rest(A)[S\sigma(n/r)|rest(R)]$ where $\mathcal{R}^* = \mathcal{R}\backslash r$ and we use the rule $\nu n.\nu m.P \equiv \nu m.\nu n.P$ to move r to the desired position.

The name r cannot be present in $rest(A)$ since it was unused in M and is thus not used to link on. Thus, we can apply the rule $\nu n.m[P] \equiv m[\nu n.P]$ if $n \neq m$ to move r below the ambient hierarchy. The resulting process $\nu\mathcal{R}^*.rest(A)[\nu r.(S\sigma(n/r)|rest(R))]$ can be transformed into $\nu\mathcal{R}^*.rest(A)[\nu r.(S\sigma(n/r))|rest(R)]$ by scope extrusion since r cannot be used in R, either.

By applying α-conversion on r we finally receive $\nu\mathcal{R}^*.rest(A)[(\nu n.S)|rest(R)]$ Since r does not appear freely in the process (in fact it does not appear there at all due to our α-conversion) we can add the restriction νr around the process to restore $\mathcal{R}$ while still maintaining the equivalence[2]. The resulting process is the desired $\nu\mathcal{R}.rest(A)[\nu n.S|rest(R)] = P_2$. □

Just like unused restricted names necessary for the processing of a restriction, unused twigs are a prerequisite for the processing of a parallel composition. We therefore prove that we can free a twig if there is a parallel composition to be processed.

Lemma 3.28 (Cutting twigs). *Let M a stable MA-PN marking. If M contains a leaf $T_u \hat{=} P|Q$ starting with a parallel composition, it either contains an unoccupied twig or can transform itself into an equivalent stable marking M' in which a twig is unused ($T_u\checkmark$).*

Proof. Since we assume a b-bounded process $R = \nu\mathcal{R}.rest(M)$ behind the marking M there is at least one process R' in R's equivalence class which does not exceed the bound b.
We can distinguish two cases:

$R = R'$: If already the best case R' which respects the bound was $\nu\mathcal{R}.rest(M)$ we already know that some unoccupied twig T_x is present: The parallel composition $P|Q$ already contributes with 2 to b in R'. The net only reserved one twig for it so far. Thus, the breadth bound b cannot be reached yet in the net and some twig T_x is marked as unused.

$R \neq R' \equiv R$: Differences in R's and R''s breadth can only origin from a different number of additional 0 leaves. These leaves' removal must really diminish the bound so that we can exclude case 2 on them. Since the net only possesses b twigs, already the removal of one unnecessary 0 will guarantee an unoccupied twig. The fact that M is associated to R already says that M is stable. Thus, either a case 1 or a case 3 transition (sequence) is enabled on the stable M. We will now show that any of them maintains stability and equivalence:

case 1: The *disappear* transition for the *root* case shown in 3.2.2.2 maintains the stability since it only tests on the semaphore. It removes some 0 on the top level transforming itself into a marking M'. That is, $R = R_1|0 \equiv R_1$ where $R_1 = \nu\mathcal{R}.rest(M')$. In the extreme case where $R_1 = \varepsilon$ the equivalence rule $0 \equiv \varepsilon$ is implemented.

case 3: Either the *at least two?* or the *ambient?* transition is enabled on the ambient a_i which also carries the 0 twig T_s. This transition now consumes the semaphore and puts a token on $yes(a_i)$ which enables the *disappear* transition shown in 3.2.2.2. In every other aspect it is a simple test so that for its result $M_0\,rest(M) = rest(M_0)$ and thus, the equivalence holds although the stability is not kept. The freshly enabled transition's firing restores the stability by putting the semaphore back. It cuts the dead twig T_s, thus implementing $K|0 \equiv K$ on some subterm K of R. This guarantees $rest(M_1) \equiv rest(M')$.

Of course, any of the above transformations marked the cut twig as unused. □

Finally we can combine the transitions which maintain the equivalence to produce an equivalent processed marking out of any stable MA-PN marking.

Lemma 3.29 (Producing processed markings). *Let M a stable MA-PN marking. M can be transformed into an equivalent processed marking M'.*

Proof. We depict how to mark forgotten restricted link names as unused first. Afterwards, we show how to remove the undesired prefixes $l[P]$, $P|Q$, and $\nu n.P$.

---

[2] The desired position in $\mathcal{R}$ can again be reached by the rule $\nu n.\nu m.P \equiv \nu m.\nu n.P$

It is sufficient to apply Lemma 3.22 (and thus transitions from 3.2.2.2) to mark any forgotten restricted name as unused while maintaining the equivalence. The necessary steps for different names may not interfere since they are working on distinct places (each place uses the link name r as reference). The concatenation of these steps will yield an equivalent marking in which each name is either in use or marked as unused.

If we perform these steps before processing any undesired prefix we can assume that each restricted link name is either really in use or marked as unused. To maintain this useful insight as an invariant we should show that no restricted link name can become unused during the execution of the subsequent steps. We will only use the transitions *split* from 3.2.2.2, $\nu n.P$ from 3.2.2.2, and $l[P]$ from 3.2.2.2 on page 33. Additional use of the 0 transformations shown in 3.2.2.2 on page 30 may be necessary but does no harm since none of them interferes with the ambient hierarchy. Only the spawner interferes with this but it only introduces a new link $a_i \mapsto l$ so that no name can be forgotten in this part. Also, no name can disappear from a leaf since we do not touch the $used(r)$ and $unused(r)$ commands which are always a name's last occurrence on a leaf.

We may start to use new names when processing a restriction but we cannot directly forget such a name with the same argumentation presented above. Thus, we can assume that each forgotten name is indeed marked as unused which will facilitate the reasoning.

With this knowledge it is easy to see that the successive removal of undesired prefixes will sooner or later lead to a processed marking. We show that this removal is indeed possible, i.e. that the corresponding transition is enabled if an undesired statement is a leaf's prefix, and that each of the removing transitions maintains the equivalence. Each prefix removing transition used below requires a test on the semaphore, which is possible since M's association to R guarantees stability. Since we only test on the semaphore the stability is also maintained by each transition.

We always assume a situation with the same names we used when introducing the transitions. In order to distinguish the marking before the transition from that afterwards, we use the names M_1 and M_2 for them.

$P|Q$: The *split* transition from Section 3.2.2.2 is enabled in the assumed situation if some unused twig T_t is present. We can apply Lemma 3.28 to guarantee such an unused twig. This may require a 0-transition leading to an intermediate marking M_1' while maintaining equivalence and stability. The *split* transition maintains the equivalence since already $rest(M_1) = rest(M_2)$ or in the case requiring an intermediate 0 transition $rest(M_1) \equiv rest(M_1') = rest(M_2)$.

$l[P]$: The $l[P]$ transition from Section 3.2.2.2 is enabled in the assumed situation if some unused ambient name a_i is present $(a_i \checkmark)$. Since we assume a b, d-bounded process unused ambient names should be present in the net since the corresponding process in which the ambient already contributes to the depth does not exceed the bound d.

This transition only allows the net to represent the old information in a more convenient way. Again, already $rest(M_1) = rest(M_2)$ holds, so that the equivalence between the markings is kept.

$\nu n.P$: The $\nu n.P$ transition from 3.2.2.2 is enabled in the assumed situation if some unused link name r is present $(r \checkmark)$. We can apply Lemma 3.26 to be sure that a name is markable as unused. With the former discussion we know that the name is already marked and thus our transition is enabled.

As we know from Lemma 3.27 the transition is a transformation within one equivalence class. □

Thus, we even have a constructive procedure to transform a marking M into an equivalent processed marking M'.

3.3.3 Bisimulation between rMA and MA-PN

We are now prepared to establish a bisimulation $M \simeq_{MA-PN} \nu \mathcal{R}.rest(M)$ between processed MA-PN markings M and their associated rMA processes $\nu \mathcal{R}.rest(M)$. We will use these exit points of each MA-PN equivalence class to mimic each possible rMA action. Afterwards MA-PN's equivalence transformations transfer the resulting marking into a new processed one. Since each action in one system is met by exactly one in the other system, the bisimulation is strong. The reader familiar with bisimulations might be interested to hear that the one proposed below is

Theorem 3.30 (Bisimulation between rMA and MA-PN). *The $(b, d$-bounded) rMA calculus and the MA-PN are bisimiliar via a strong bisimulation $M_p \simeq_{MA-PN} \nu \mathcal{R}.rest(M_p)$ for processed MA-PN markings M_p.*

Proof. We limit our analysis to processed MA-PN markings. These markings are sufficient to express every equivalence class $[M]_{\equiv_{MA-PN}}$ since an arbitrary marking M can be transformed into an equivalent one in processed form as stated by Lemma 3.29.

Processed markings are stable. Thus, we can contract several Petri net transitions, which lead from one stable marking over intermediate unstable markings into another stable marking, into one MA-PN action. They are then considered atomic for the bisimulation. The most prominent case is the *open* action which uses a blocking chain of transitions to reinstall a correct tree.

We do not consider equivalence transformations as actions, neither for rMA nor for MA-PN. A Petri net transition which simply performs an equivalence transformation could anyway be mimicked by an ε action in rMA. We will use these transitions implicitly when transforming the resulting marking of an action into an equivalent processed one. The remaining MA-PN actions are **call** (3.2.2.1 on page 28), **used** (3.2.2.1 on page 29), **unused** (3.2.2.1 on page 29), **in** (3.2.2.1 on page 26), **out** (3.2.2.1 on page 27), and **open**. We contract the original *open l.P* transition shown in 3.2.2.1 and its succeeding chain of *release* and *test* transitions also shown in 3.2.2.1 to this action. The intermediate transitions are only executed if the semaphore is not present since *open l.P* consumed it and only the last transition of the chain restores it. We establish the bisimulation $M \simeq_{MA-PN} \nu\mathcal{R}.rest(M)$ between a processed MA-PN marking M and its associated rMA process $\nu\mathcal{R}.rest(M)$. This also shows $[\nu\mathcal{R}.rest(M)]_{\equiv_{MA-PN}} [M]_{\equiv_{PN}}$.

Fact 1 *For a pair $P \in rMA$ and $Q \in MA - PN$ with $P \simeq_{MA-PN} Q$, whenever $P \leadsto^\alpha P' \in rMA$, there is $Q' \in MA - PN$ such that $Q \Rightarrow^{\widehat{\alpha}} Q'$ and $(P', Q') \in \simeq_{MA-PN}$.*

Proof. We formerly pointed out that arbitrary markings are not always able to perform the same actions their associated rMA process can perform. However, an equivalent processed marking can execute exactly these actions since only silent actions, calls and capabilities form the leaf prefixes.

Thus, each associated processed MA-PN marking Q can mimic its rMA process P's actions by the MA-PN action with the same name. However, the MA-PN marking after the action's execution could be in unprocessed form but we can transfer it into an equivalent processed one by applying Lemma 3.29. □

Thus, we can turn our attention to the other direction. Again, we will see that the simulation is strong so that we indeed receive a strong bisimulation between rMA and MA-PN.

Fact 2 *For a pair $Q \in MA - PN$ and $P \in rMA$ with $P \simeq_{MA-PN} Q$, whenever $Q \leadsto^\alpha Q' \in MA - PN$, there is $P' \in rMA$ such that $P \Rightarrow^{\widehat{\alpha}} P'$ and $(P', Q') \in \simeq_{MA-PN}$.*

Proof. Q performs a real action before if necessary restoring processed form. This action can be mimicked by the same action in P's form in a strong sense, that is without intermediate silent actions. In fact, rMA's silent actions are matched exactly by the *used(r)* or *unused(r)* MA-PN action.

It is interesting to see that a (strong) simulation could also be established between an arbitrary (possibly unprocessed) marking Q and its associated rMA process P. If Q contains unprocessed restrictions, parallel compositions or ambients this hinders the thus covered capability or *(un)used* action. This even reduces the challenge for rMA which is now only forced to execute the remaining, uncovered actions. As discussed before, the congruence guarantees that it can execute all actions which are not covered by a capability or silent action anyway. □

The two (strong) simulations guarantee a bisimulation between rMA and MA-PN. □

We can combine the bisimulation between MA and rMA and that between rMA and MA-PN to receive the following theorem:

Theorem 3.31. *The b, d-bounded MA processes and MA-PN are weakly bisimiliar.*

Proof. We combine Lemma 3.3 and Theorem 3.30 via the transitivity of bisimulations given by Lemma 1.10 to receive a bisimulation between b, d-bounded MA and MA-PN. It links MA process terms P to processed markings M via the intermediate step over the rMA process terms $pre(P)$. □

We derived a constructive procedure to build a bisimiliar Safe Petri net for any b, d-bounded MA process P: First we calculate the rMA process $pre(P)$, then we construct MA-PN$(pre(P))$.

Chapter 4
Further Remarks

We conclude this work by discussing how to improve the analysis of MA processes with the insights that we gained. The relaxed semantics proposed in Section 4.1.1 provides interesting approaches for future work by allowing a divide and conquer approach to the decision of MA reachability. The idea is applicable to an (r)MA term as well as to an MA-PN marking. Section 4.1.2 extends the bisimilarity to arbitrary MA processes and the reachability results for b, d-bounded processes to bounded runs of unbounded processes and shows an examplary usage.

We then address simple improvements of the construction, namely the decoupling of spread value change and twig in Section 4.1.3 and the avoidance of public names in calls in Section 4.1.4, before we summarise the construction and its benefit in Section 4.2. We close the main part of this work with a reference to those ideas we could not yet incorporate here but which we believe to be important to address in the future.

4.1 Extensions and Optimisation

We discuss modifications which are based on further insights into MA's mechanisms and facilitate verification. A relaxed approach towards the MA semantics shown in Section 4.1.1 can allow us to detect unaccessible ambients early: If the restricted link name of an ambient is only used in the inner tree but forgotten among all leaves we can conclude that the ambient is garbage. It must remain in the tree structure but cannot be accessed any more. A sibling-free parent child relation of two garbage ambients effectively hinders any communication between the lower and the upper tree so that we can divide the verification problem into two much smaller ones.

We enlarge our translation to arbitrary unbounded MA processes in Section 4.1.2. Artificial bounds allow us to extend the reachability analysis to those runs of infinite processes which respect the bounds of a finite net. An example illustrates that such a simulation can be sufficient to capture important behavioural aspects. There are other simple changes which save transitions or places like the modularisation approach in Section 4.1.3 and the banning of public names from parameter lists introduced in Section 4.1.4. Also, we can drop complement places on the *root* and avoid the test on the semaphore in transitions which do not interfere with the ambient hierarchy. This is especially helpful if one uses a verification tool which works best with concurrency.

4.1.1 Relaxed MA Semantics

We can save a considerable amount of link names and prepare the way for further optimisations if we take a relaxed approach towards the semantics. The idea is based on the fact that an ambient's link will never be changed if the corresponding link name is forgotten among all leaves: The only way to change an ambient's link is to *open*, that is remove, it and afterwards assign it in a new spawn. As soon as the link name is forgotten among all leaves, no capability on it will be executed. Thus, any ambient linked to it remains as some kind of garbage, blocking other ambients from passing in certain constellations. Such properties are also detectable without the MA-PN since the leaves of a process term can be inspected to see whether a name is forgotten among all leaves.

A border of two sibling-less *garbage* ambients above each other blocks the tree below from that above and thus separates the verification problems.

Example 4.1 (Separating verification problems). A border of two *garbage* ambients makes the execution of *out m* and *in n* impossible:

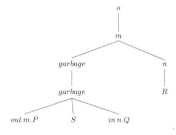

Fig. 4.1 No action in R or the above may interfere with the tree under *garbage* so that the subtrees can never interact.

Indeed, we can treat the process terms $out\,m.P|S|in\,n.Q$ and $o[mn[[R]]]$ separately so that the problems are much smaller.

To implement the relaxed semantics in the net only the *test* procedure from Section 3.2.2.2 must be adapted: We now relink the forgotten ambients onto the additional link name *garbage*. This allows the procedure to go on where it formerly blocked. Thus, a link name r can be released as soon as it is forgotten among all leaves. This changes the according actions in the possible situations for the *test* procedure – which is now in fact a *release* procedure – to:

- $a_*\checkmark$: The ambient name a_* is currently unused. In this case we do not need to change the linking since there is no relevant link installed but can immediately proceed to a_{*+1}.
- $a_* \mapsto r$: If a_* was so far linked onto r we must replace this link by one onto *garbage* before proceeding to a_{*+1}.
- $a_* \mapsto x \neq r$: If a_* is linked onto a name different to r or already linked onto *garbage* there is no need to touch the relation. Thus, we can immediately proceed to a_{*+1}.

Thus, there are two new transitions per ambient a_*. We need an extra test on the artificial name *garbage* and we add a transition for the formerly blocking $a_* \mapsto r$ case. This new transition is the only one changing the link relation since it relinks the ambient from r onto *garbage*.

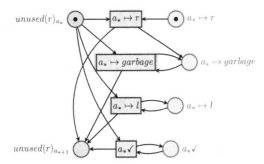

The complexity class of the number of transitions is not touched. The additional two transitions per ambient a_* with fixed link name r vanish among the $\mathcal{O}(|\mathcal{L}|)$ many transitions which are anyway used in each such constellation. Thus, the overall complexity is not affected either so that we have $\mathcal{O}(|\mathcal{A}| \cdot |\mathcal{R}| \cdot |\mathcal{L}|)$ transitions over all possible ambient names a_* and restricted link names $r \in \mathcal{R}$.

Since restricted link names which are only referenced by ambients can be freed now we only need $b \cdot (c + \kappa)$ restricted link names instead of the former $b \cdot (c + \kappa) + d$ many names. Even more interesting than this considerable saving of names and places is the potential to separate verification problems.

4.1.2 Simulation of Unbounded Processes

It is easy to see that the construction allows us to simulate finite runs of unbounded processes, too, if we additionally provide a transition for the unbounded replication. Even though this element guarantees infinite breadth, already a finite number of its replicants may reveal interesting behaviour. The replication implements $!P \equiv P \,|\, !P$. The behaviour and thus the required Petri net transition is hence quite similar to that for the parallel composition $P|Q$ as shown in Section 3.2.2.2. Again, we use a_i as parent ambient, T_s as already used twig and T_t as freshly occupied one.

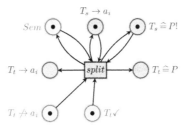

The only difference to the former transition lies in the fact that $!P$ is kept as T_s's content while $P|Q$ was split. The test on $!P$ is necessary to make sure that the P replication is present. In order to implement all necessary equivalence rules to keep the process representation small in breadth we care for $!0 \equiv 0$. It translates to:

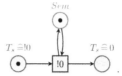

This makes $\mathcal{O}(|\mathbb{T}|)$ many transitions. In fact, we do not even need the semaphore here since the transition doesn't interfere with the tree structure.

This second transition guarantees that our b, d-bounded MA-PN with replication indeed simulates all b, d-bounded runs. We can even take a further step towards generality: The bisimulation extends to arbitrary runs and processes if we consider possibly infinite Petri nets with replication transitions (MA-PN$_{repli}$). In fact, the proof becomes much simpler since we can always assume an unused name of the respective, now infinite name set. The difficult freeing of restricted link names is no more necessary then.

Theorem 4.2 (Extended bisimulation between rMA and MA-PN$_{repli}$). *The rMA calculus and the MA-PN$_{repli}$ are bisimilar via* $M_p \simeq_{MA-PN} \nu\mathcal{R}.rest(M_p)$ *for processed MA-PN$_{repli}$ markings M_p.*

Proof. The proof mimics that of Theorem 3.30 with an additional case for the unbounded replication whenever we considered the parallel compostion. It is analysed in complete analogy. □

Based on this insight we can derive the following characterisation:

Theorem 4.3 (Finiteness iff bounded). *Let P an rMA process. The MA-PN$_{repli}(P)$ is finite iff P is b, d-bounded.*

Proof. Finiteness of the net is only possible if the process is bounded in breadth and depth. If the process is bounded we can compile a finite MA-PN$_{repli}$ for it by using the true b and d as bounds. □

This nice characterisation is not applicable in practice at all. We will therefore withdraw from infinite Petri nets and show in an example how to simulate interesting runs with given artificial breadth and depth bounds.
   We consider the process $(P_{\llcorner\lrcorner} = \nu m.(n[open\, m.P] \mid m[in\, n.0]), P)$. The public name n is the only one so that our link name set is $\mathcal{L} = \{n\} \cup \mathcal{R}$. We have $c = 1$ and $k = 0$ so that we only need $b \cdot 1 + d$ many restricted link names. Instead of computing the bounds we set $b = 2$ and $d = 3$. Thus, our other associated MA-PN sets are $\mathbb{T} = \{T_1, T_2\}$, $\mathcal{A} = \{a_1, \ldots, a_3\}$, and $\mathcal{R} = \{r_1, \ldots, r_5\}$. To determine the associated set of buds we must apply the preprocessing first. It yields the modified process equation $P_{\llcorner\lrcorner} = \nu m.used(m).(n[open\, m.unused(m).P] \mid m[unused(m).in\, n.0])$. The buds are

$$\{\nu m.used(m).(n[open\, m.unused(m).P] \mid m[unused(m).in\, n.0])\}$$
$$\cup\; \{used(r_i).(n[open\, r_i.unused(r_i).P] \mid r_i[unused(r_i).in\, n.0]),$$
$$n[open\, r_i.unused(r_i).P] \mid r_i[unused(r_i).in\, n.0],$$
$$n[open\, r_i.unused(r_i).P], \; r_i[unused(r_i).in\, n.0],$$
$$open\, r_i.unused(r_i).P, \; unused(r_i).in\, n.0,$$
$$unused(r_i).P, \; in\, n.0 \mid i = 1, \ldots, 5\}$$
$$\cup\; \{P, 0\}.$$

This modest size parameters already yield a large net which we will not depict here. Instead, we show a run and thus only those transitions which are used.

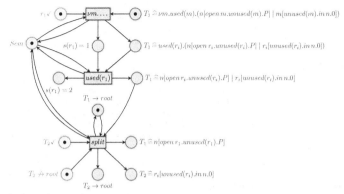

So far, only a *used* action took place, the other two transitions were equivalence transformations. The respective MA-PN tree is:

$$root$$

$$T_1 \mathrel{\hat{=}} n[open\, r_1.unused(r_1).P] \qquad T_2 \mathrel{\hat{=}} r_1[unused(r_1).in\, n.0]$$

We need to integrate the ambients into the tree before we process the next actions. We omit the semaphore in the *unused* transition due to readability. Both ambient spawners are concurrent. One is shown above the other transitions and the other one is depicted leftmost. After both fired we can process $unused(r_1)$ to finally enable *in* n.

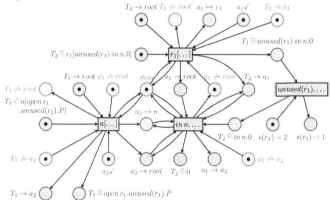

The process state after the execution of all four transitions is:

$$root$$
$$|$$
$$a_2(\mapsto n)$$

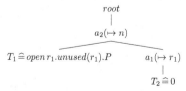

After the three transitions fired the *open* capability can be executed. Afterwards, 0 can be removed so that we free T_2. The twig T_1 is now a_2's only child:

$$
\begin{array}{ccc}
root & & root \\
| & & | \\
a_2(\mapsto n) & \rightsquigarrow MA{-}PN & a_2(\mapsto n) \\
| & & | \\
T_1 \mathrel{\widehat{=}} unused(r_1).P & & T_1 \mathrel{\widehat{=}} P
\end{array}
$$

The execution of the last *unused* transition removes the spread count and allows us to free r_1. This restores the initial state only with an additional n ambient named a_2. Thus, we can conclude that our process is unbounded in depth. Since its behaviour is quite limited we can easily check that its breadth is indeed bounded by 2. If we continue the simulation we can watch the chain of n ambients grow. There is no further behaviour. Thus, the very limited simulation was sufficient to understand the whole process behaviour and derive its true bounds.

4.1.3 Saving Transitions by Modularisation

The $(un)use$ transition for a restricted link name r is implemented per spread value $s(r)$. We can replace this spread value dependent *unused* action by a small procedure: The first transition consumes the semaphore and puts a token on the respective operation: $decrem(r)$ for $unused(r)$ and $increm(r)$ for the $use(r)$ action.

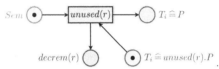

Now we need one transition per bud $unused(r).P$ and twig T_i which is in $\mathcal{O}(|\mathbb{B}| \cdot |\mathbb{T}|)$ and saves a factor of $2 \cdot b$ in comparison to the former transition. In a second step we perform the spread change:

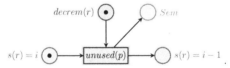

Even with these additional $(2 \cdot b) \cdot |\mathcal{R}|$ transitions the procedure is less expensive: Since $|\mathbb{B}| \gg |\mathcal{R}|$ the new sequences overall require $\mathcal{O}(|\mathbb{B}| \cdot b)$ many transitions.

4.1.4 Excluding Public Names from Parameter Lists

The behaviour of calls in the MA calculus is static in almost every aspect. This is mostly due to the fact that there is no name passing mechanism like the *send* and *receive* actions in the π-calculus. In MA a name may only by passed by using it as a call parameter for a subsequent equation.

There are three types of names a process can choose from when calling other process equations:

- public names $p \in \mathcal{P}$
- own freshly spawned restricted names $r \in \mathcal{R}$
- own parameters $x \in \mathcal{L}$, i.e. names the process received from its parent (via the former call), which can be either restricted or public

However, explicitly called public names can be eliminated: If we have an equation – including the initial term – which calls the process equation $P(\vec{y})$ with the public name $a \in \mathcal{P}$ as i-th parameter, we can transform $P(\vec{y})$ into an equation $P_a(y_1, \ldots, y_{i-1}, y_{i+1}, \ldots, y_n)$ which does not use a as explicit parameter but already comes with the substitution of x_i by a, that is $P_a = P\sigma(x_i/a)$. Applying this to all public names in every equation successively, we receive equations which may only pass newly restricted names or own parameters to any sibling. By induction, it follows that no process need pass public names as parameters at all, thus leaving us only to deal with two types of names: Own freshly restricted names $r \in \mathcal{R}$ and own parameters $x \in \mathcal{R}$, i.e. restricted names the process received from its parent.

The shorter parameter list and the banning of public names from calls come at the price of many more equations. For example, if there are only three calls $P(a)$, $P(b)$, and $P(c)$ on three different public names a, b, and c this was formerly handled by one process equation $P\llcorner x \lrcorner$. Now we need three parameterless equations P_a, P_b, and P_c. However, we eliminate some peculiarities from our MA-PN if we require processes not to use public names as parameters. For example, we can drop the transitions eliminating $(un)use$ commands on public names and we can shorten the substitution net introduced in Appendix B.

4.2 Conclusion and Future Work

We presented a polynomial construction to compile a Safe Petri net with equivalent behaviour for a given b, d-bounded MA process P. This guarantees PSPACE-complete decidability of reachability, liveness, and persistence for P.

Crucial for our construction was an efficient name management which guaranteed uniqueness of the encoded process term for recovery on one hand and allowed for quick reuse of names on the other hand. We accomplished this task by maintaining each name's spread among leaf process terms and a checking procedure to determine use in the ambient tree. As soon as a name wasn't present in the process any more we allowed the net to reuse it. We therefore invented a preprocessing which added the necessary $(un)use$ commands to adjust the spread to our process terms. Since these commands extended MA's syntax we defined the refined MA calculus (rMA) incorporating them.

Our construction highlights MA's "heart", that is those principles and design decisions that make it work the way it does. We established a clear distinction between the ambient tree and leaf process terms by separating them via twigs. The distinction extends onto the names, too, by a separation between ambient names $\mathcal{A}$, that uniquely represent an ambient in the tree, and link names $\mathcal{L}$, which occur in leaves only and partition the ambient tree.

This separation does not only allow the Petri net to maintain a unique tree but also reveals an important peculiarity of MA: Names which are only used in the ambient tree but do not appear on the leaves any more cannot be addressed by capabilities. Thus, their ambients remain as some kind of $garbage$ in the tree. As first examples show, some constellations of them disrupt the tree since $garbage$ levels cannot be accessed and thus hurdled. This allows us to divide (and hopefully conquer) larger verification problems. Although we only proposed it in the context of our Petri nets the technique to identify the $garbage$ names is not limited to our translation but may already be applied to the original process. It is an open question to discover further constellations which guarantee disruption. Also, we should examine how one can integrate the identification of these break points into existing verification tools, e.g. into model checkers based on Ambient logic ([CG00]).

Promising saving potential comes from some insight in the static behaviour of calls. It is interesting to see that a call from a given process equation to the same sibling always happens with the same freshly restricted names. The reason is that this call is hard-coded in the first process's own equation. While the own restricted names are thus always the same, some variation seems to come from the equation's own parameters. But since all of the equations experience this effect we can inductively conclude that the own parameters' influence is also static – although static in a larger sense. This should allow us to determine a static call graph which already reveals most of the possible process behaviour. First analyses indicate two ways in which names propagate in this graph. Names appearing twice over several call iterations at the same parameter position persist while other names take some hops and then fade out. This seems to allow for acceleration in the way of the Karp and Miller algorithm for Petri net coverability ([KM69]) on arbitrary MA processes.

As we showed, the principles behind MA are quite different to those behind its ancestor, the π-calculus. While the $send$ and $receive$ actions incorporated in the latter calculus allow an unpredictable dynamic assignment of names, MA's name propagation is statically determined. [CG98] proposed an extension of the pure MA calculus with π's communication primitives which allows for a convenient encoding of arbitrary π-calculus processes. The difference in pure MA's and π's behaviour gives rise to the idea that this extension's expressive power is higher. But even the pure MA calculus was proven Turing-complete ([CG98]) which contradicts this conjecture. Thus, the additional dynamics of the extension can add no power. It is natural to investigate whether some of these dynamics can be avoided, thus faciliating π-calculus verification or whether the same dynamics are contained in MA in some hidden form.

Appendix A
Transition Summary

We depict all MA-PN transitions of Section 3.2.2 with their respective purposes but without any explanation or analysis. This appendix is designed for quick readers who want to skip the explanatory introduction of the transitions and for those who wish to check the proofs of Section 3.3. The used instance names are therefore the same as those in construction and proof. Additionally, the structure of the construction is exactly met: We divide the appendix into two Sections of which the first is dedicated to transition (chains) that form actions and the second part to the equivalence transformations.

A.1 Summary: The MA-PN Transitions

We use distinct identifiers out of the associated MA-PN sets, namely $T_s, T_t \in \mathbb{T}$, $a_i, a_j, a_k \in \mathcal{A}$, $l \in \mathcal{L}$, $r \in \mathcal{R}$, and $p \in \mathcal{P}$ which are the same used in Section 3.2.2. In the case of the *open* test chain we iterate over all ambient names so that we additionally use a_d to indicate the chain's last element. The transition $a_* \mapsto \mathcal{L} \setminus \{r\}$ stands for the set of similar transitions for each element in $\mathcal{L} \setminus \{r\}$ per fixed restricted link name r and varying but per set fixed ambient a_*.

A.1.1 Transitions for rMA Actions

In:

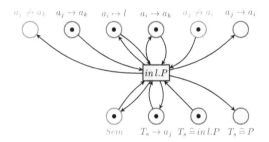

Out:

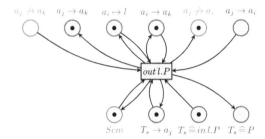

Open:

$M = \mathbb{T} \cup (\mathcal{A} \setminus \{a_i, a_j\})$, $|M| = m = b + (c + \kappa) \cdot b + d - 2$

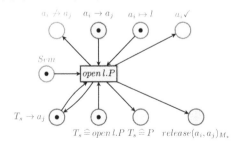

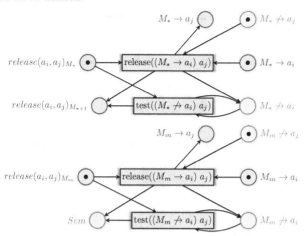

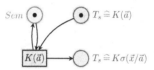

Call:

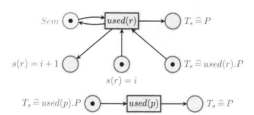

Used:

$1 \leq i \leq 2 \cdot b$

Unused:

$2 \leq i \leq 2 \cdot b$

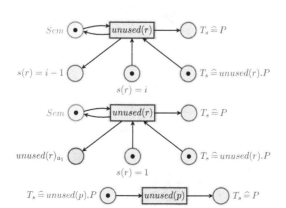

A.1.2 Transitions for Equivalence Transformations

Test Chain:

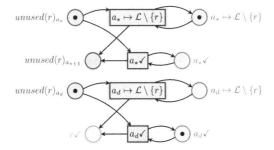

Spawn:

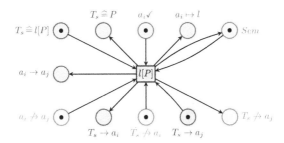

Restriction:

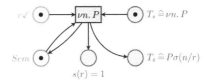

0 Removal:

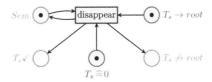

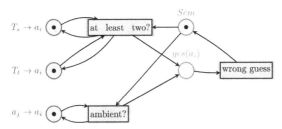

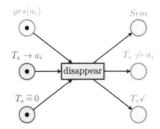

Parallel Composition:

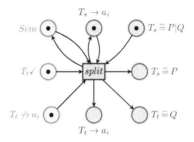

Appendix B
Polynomial Construction Using a Substitution Net

In this chapter we introduce the final complete construction that additionally uses a substitution net [MKH12] that guarantees a reduction of b, d-bounded MA to safe Petri nets that is polynomial in the process size and the bounds.

In Section B.1 we show the modified buds that now simply stick to the original names and apply no substitutions any more. This original MA name and the twig which the bud belongs to are enough to uniquely determine the implied restriction. That is then connected to a restricted link name via a substitution place that is fed as soon as we process the restriction. We show the implication of the substitution net on our construction in Section B.2, that is we give all transitions whose formulation now changes.

B.1 The New Buds

The representation of all possible substitutions made the set of buds exponential in the former construction. Now we can stick to the original (r)MA names and maintain the connection to the link name in the substitution net. For the set of buds we thus have:

Definition B.1 (MA-PN set of buds). Let $\mathbb{P} = (D, I)$ an rMA process with $D = \{D_1, \dots, D_n\}$, $\vec{x}_i$ the list of formal parameters for the defining equation D_i, and $\vec{a} \in fn(D_i) \cup rn(D_i)$ the actual parameters. We define $\mathbb{B} := b(I) \cup \bigcup_{i=1}^{n} b(D_i)$ where

$$b(0) := \{0\} \qquad\qquad\qquad b(D_i(\vec{a})) := \{D_i(\vec{a})\}$$
$$b(\pi.P) := \{\pi.P\} \cup b(P) \qquad\qquad b(n[P]) := \{n[P]\} \cup b(P)$$
$$b(![P]) := \{![P]\} \cup b(P) \qquad\qquad b(\nu n.P) := \{\nu n.P\} \cup b(P)$$
$$b(P \,|\, Q) := \{P \,|\, Q\} \cup b(P) \cup b(Q) \qquad\qquad b(\tau.P) := \{\tau.P\} \cup b(P)$$

One can easily see that each equation now only produces $\mathcal{O}(D_i)$ many buds which keeps $|\mathbb{B}| \in \mathcal{O}(n)$. Also, we need not define the associated sets $\mathcal{R}$, $\mathcal{P}$, and $\mathcal{L}$ in advance.

B.2 The Substitution Net

We will log a substitution for each leaf and thus bind it to the respective twig. Since we process a call only if it is the only remaining element on a leaf, we never need more than the formal parameters and new restrictions of one equation. To keep the number of additional places small we assume that each equation D_i uses the formal parameters x_1 to x_{k_i} so that there are only κ formal parameters x_1 to x_κ over all equations. Also, each equation should use the restrictions c_1 to c_{c_i} which gives us c_1 to c_c. We unite these MA names under the name set $N = \{x_i | i = 1, \dots, \kappa\} \cup \{c_i | i = 1, \dots, c\}$.

We distinguish the names $n \in N$ on different leaf terms by additionally referencing the twig. Thus, we have new places $T_s : n = l$ for $T_s \in \mathbb{T}$, $n \in N$, and $l \in \mathcal{L}$ as well as the complement place $T_s : n = \emptyset$ per name $n \in N$ and twig T_s.

B.2.1 Influence on Capabilities and Silent Actions

We use $in\,n.P$ as an example to illustrate the effect on capabilities and silent actions. Since we do not replace MA names any more the original name $n \in N$ remains. The connection between the ambient and the action is now managed by two relations $a_i \mapsto l$ linking the ambient a_i to the link name $l \in \mathcal{L}$, and $T_s : n = l$ which links the name n written in the action to l.

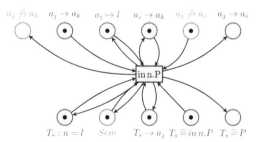

There is now one transition per ambient name a_i, a_j, and a_k, twig T_s, link name l, and bud $in\,n.P$ which contains an additional factor $|\mathcal{L}|$ compared to what we had before: There are now $\mathcal{O}(|\mathcal{A}| \cdot |\mathcal{A}| \cdot |\mathcal{A}| \cdot |\mathcal{L}| \cdot |\mathbb{T}| \cdot |\mathbb{B}|)$ many transitions but now $|\mathbb{B}| \in \mathcal{O}(n)$ so that we save a considerable amount of transitions.

B.2.2 Ambient Spawn

When translating a spawn we now use a test on $T_s : n = l$ to determine the correct link name l. Since each name is only used once within an equation due to NC and each twig T_s is only inherited by a part of one equation the connection is unique.

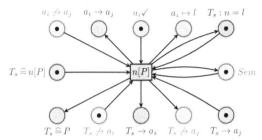

One can easily see that the additional test on $T_s : n = l$ again adds a factor $|\mathcal{L}|$ but the reduction on $|\mathbb{B}|$ amortises this.

B.2.3 The Restriction

We establish a new substitution whenever we process a restriction νc. We make sure that only substitutions for those names which are passed on as parameters are kept at a call. They are then migrated to the parameters $\vec{x}$ and all substitutions on $\vec{c}$ are removed so that NC guarantees that we have no link on c if there is a new restriction on it.

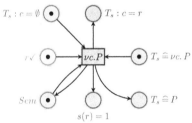

We need one transition per bud $\nu c.P$, twig T_s and chosen restricted link name r, thus $\mathcal{O}\left(|\mathbb{B}| \cdot |\mathbb{T}| \cdot |\mathcal{R}|\right)$ many transitions.

B.2.4 The Parallel Composition

Whenever we process a parallel composition $T_s \cong P|Q$ we occupy a second twig T_t. Thus, we need to copy the substitution information from T_s to T_t. We decided against flushing T_t's substitution when freeing it $(T_t\checkmark)$ so that an arbitrary substitution may be stored on T_t when we assign Q to it. Thus, we must flush it before setting the new substitution.

The former *split* transition now additionally fills initiator places for flush $(flush_{T_t}(1))$ and copy $(copy_{(T_s,T_t)}(1))$. The latter is necessary to log for *store* which twig T_t to copy T_s's substitutions to without transporting this information through the *flush*.

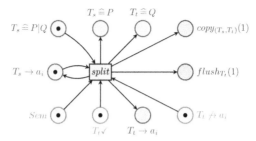

The *split* transition's former number is not changed. We flush T_t's substitutions using $flush_{T_t}(1)$ as initiator. For each number * from this 1 until $c + \kappa$ we perform:

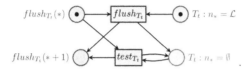

We need $|\mathcal{L}|$ many *flush* transitions and an additional *test* transition for fixed name n_* and twig T_t. With $c + \kappa$ many names n_* this makes $\mathcal{O}\left(|\mathcal{L}| \cdot (c + \kappa) \cdot |\mathbf{T}|\right)$ many transitions over all *flush* chains. The chain's last transition sets $flushed_{T_t}$ to state that T_t's former substitutions are all removed. We consume this information at the beginning of the *copy* chain. With it we set all the substitutions T_s maintains for T_t, too. We again iterate over all names since we must check all possible restrictions and paramters of T_s.

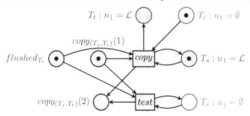

All other transitions simply consume $copy_{T_s,T_t}(*)$ (and no additional $flushed_{T_t}$). At the end of the chain we have $* = c + \kappa$ and we reset the semaphore instead of setting $copy_{(T_s,T_t)}(*+1)$. Again, these slight changes do not influence the number of transitions we need in each step of the chain. There is one *copy* transition per link name $\mathcal{L}$ and an additional *test* for fixed twig combination T_s, T_t and name n_* so that we have $\mathcal{O}\left(|\mathcal{L}| \cdot |\mathbf{T}| \cdot |\mathbf{T}| \cdot (c + \kappa)\right)$ many transitions.

B.2.5 The Call

Calls now require a complex – but still polynomial – procedure. We intermediately store the old substitution in order to avoid races. These could happen when we set the new substitution for x_j but require x_j's former value to set a later parameter x_k. While saving the old values we also completely flush the substitution on the respective twig T_s. Afterwards we set the new values for x_1 to x_{k_i} and finally flush the intermediate storage.

B.2.5.1 Call Step

The actual call now fills to additional places $store_{T_s}(1)$ and $set(a_n \ldots a_1)$ and consumes the semaphore rather than only testing on it. The $store_{T_s}(1)$ initiates the storing of the old substitution while $set(a_n \ldots a_1)$ maintains the actual parameters for the setting of the new substitution on $\vec{x}$.

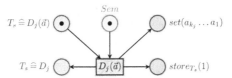

The bud $D_j(\vec{a})$ and the used twig T_s together determine the call step completely. We thus only have $|\mathbb{B}| \cdot |\mathbb{T}|$ many call transitions.

B.2.5.2 Storing the Old Substitution and Flushing It on the Twig

We implement a chain over N which stores the connection between T_s's name n_* and a link name if there is one, and simply proceeds, if there is none ($T_s : n_* = \emptyset$). The flushing of the old substitution is already integrated by emptying $T_s : n_* = l$ and filling $T_s : n_* = \emptyset$.

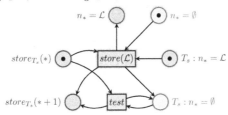

Per name n_* and twig T_s we need $|\mathcal{L}|$ many *store* transitions and one *test* transition. This makes $\mathcal{O}((c + \kappa) \cdot |\mathbb{T}| \cdot |\mathcal{L}|)$ many transitions over all names n_1 to $n_{c+\kappa}$ and twigs $T_s \in \mathbb{T}$. We may again modify the last transition to fill the next chain's initiator set_{T_s} rather than $store_{T_s}(c + \kappa + 1)$.

B.2.5.3 Setting the New Substitution

The *set* procedure links the stored old substitution with the actually called parameters maintained on $set(a_{k_j} \ldots a_1)$ in order to determine the new values for $\vec{x}$. The test on set_{T_s} is not only necessary to guarantee that store and flush are done but also to determine the correct twig T_s. We use the reverse parameter vector starting with x_{k_j} since the remaining number of parameters, $*$, then corresponds to the name x_* for which we should set the substitution next.

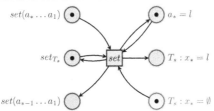

Each *set* transitions' target x_* is determined by the length $*$ of $a_* \ldots a_1$, which is bound by κ. Thus, each chain may only consist of up to κ many transitions. Over all twigs T_s, link names l, and possible start combinations $\vec{a}$, whose number is bound by $|\mathbb{B}|$, we thus have $\mathcal{O}(|\mathbb{T}| \cdot |\mathcal{L}| \cdot |\mathbb{B}| \cdot \kappa)$ many transitions.

The last transition consumes set_{T_s} rather than testing on it. Also, it sets $flush_{store}(1)$ instead of $set()$ to prepare for the flushing of the intermediate store:

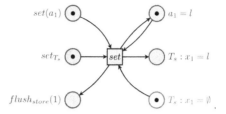

B.2.5.4 Flushing the Intermediate Storage

This last N iterator removes any intermediately stored link $n_* = \mathcal{L}$. Per fixed name n_* each link name is considered. The last transition set can finally restore the semaphore.

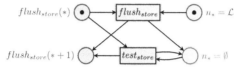

Per name n_* and twig T_s we again need $|\mathcal{L}|$ many $flush_{store}$ transitions and one $test_{store}$ transition. This makes $\mathcal{O}((c + \kappa) \cdot |\mathbb{T}| \cdot |\mathcal{L}|)$ many transitions over all names and twigs.

References

[BZ09]   Nadia Busi and Gianluigi Zavattaro. Deciding reachability problems in turing-complete fragments of mobile
           ambients. *Mathematical Structures in Computer Science*, 19:1223–1263, 12 2009.
[CEP95]   Allan Cheng, Javier Esparza, and Jens Palsberg. Complexity results for 1-safe nets. *Theor. Comput. Sci.*,
           147(1&2):117–136, 1995.
[CG98]   Luca Cardelli and Andrew D. Gordon. Mobile ambients. In Maurice Nivat, editor, *Foundations of Software Sci-
           ence and Computation Structures*, volume 1378 of *Lecture Notes in Computer Science*, pages 140–155. Springer
           Berlin Heidelberg, 1998.
[CG00]   Luca Cardelli and Andrew D. Gordon. Anytime, anywhere: modal logics for mobile ambients. In *Proceedings
           of the 27th ACM SIGPLAN-SIGACT symposium on Principles of programming languages*, POPL '00, pages
           365–377, New York, NY, USA, 2000. ACM.
[CZG+01]   Witold Charatonik, Silvano Zilio, AndrewD. Gordon, Supratik Mukhopadhyay, and Jean-Marc Talbot. The
           complexity of model checking mobile ambients. In Furio Honsell and Marino Miculan, editors, *Foundations
           of Software Science and Computation Structures*, volume 2030 of *Lecture Notes in Computer Science*, pages
           152–167. Springer Berlin Heidelberg, 2001.
[Dam96]   Mads Dam. Model checking mobile processes. *Information and Computation*, 129(1):35 – 51, 1996.
[EN94]   Javier Esparza and Mogens Nielsen. Decidability issues for petri nets - a survey. *Bulletin of the EATCS*,
           52:244–262, 1994.
[GC03]   Andrew D. Gordon and Luca Cardelli. Equational properties of mobile ambients. *Mathematical Structures in
           Computer Science*, 13(3):371–408, 2003.
[KK06]   Barbara König and Vitali Kozioura. Counterexample-guided abstraction refinement for the analysis of graph
           transformation systems. In Holger Hermanns and Jens Palsberg, editors, *TACAS*, volume 3920 of *Lecture Notes
           in Computer Science*, pages 197–211. Springer, 2006.
[KM69]   Richard M. Karp and Raymond E. Miller. Parallel program schemata. *Journal of Computer and System Sciences*,
           3(2):147 – 195, 1969.
[LS03]   Francesca Levi and Davide Sangiorgi. Mobile safe ambients. *ACM Trans. Program. Lang. Syst.*, 25(1):1–69,
           January 2003.
[Mey08]   Roland Meyer. On boundedness in depth in the pi-calculus. In *In Procedings of IFIP TCS 2008*, volume 273 of
           IFIP, pages 477–489. Springer, 2008.
[Mey09]   Roland Meyer. A theory of structural stationarity in the pi-calculus. *Acta Informatica*, 46(2):87–137, 2009.
[MG09]   Roland Meyer and Roberto Gorrieri. On the relationship between pi-calculus and finite place/transition petri
           nets. In *In Procedings of CONCUR 2009*, volume 5710 of *LNCS*, pages 463–480. Springer, 2009.
[MH02]   Massimo Merro and Matthew Hennessy. Bisimulation congruences in safe ambients. In *Proceedings of the 29th
           ACM SIGPLAN-SIGACT symposium on Principles of programming languages*, POPL '02, pages 71–80, New
           York, NY, USA, 2002. ACM.
[Mil89]   R. Milner. *Communication and concurrency*. Prentice-Hall, Inc., Upper Saddle River, NJ, USA, 1989.
[Mil99]   Robin Milner. *Communicating and mobile systems - the Pi-calculus*. Cambridge University Press, 1999.
[MKH12]   Roland Meyer, Victor Khomenko, and Reiner Hüchting. A polynomial translation of pi-calculus (fcp) to safe
           petri nets. In Maciej Koutny and Irek Ulidowski, editors, *CONCUR 2012 – Concurrency Theory*, volume 7454
           of *Lecture Notes in Computer Science*, pages 440–455. Springer Berlin Heidelberg, 2012.
[MKS08]   Roland Meyer, Victor Khomenko, and Tim Strazny. A practical approach to verification of mobile systems using
           net unfoldings. In KeesM. Hee and Rüdiger Valk, editors, *Applications and Theory of Petri Nets*, volume 5062
           of *Lecture Notes in Computer Science*, pages 327–347. Springer Berlin Heidelberg, 2008.
[MP05]   Sergio Maffeis and Iain Phillips. On the computational strength of pure ambient calculi. *Theoretical Computer
           Science*, 2005.
[Oqu04]   Flavio Oquendo. Pi-adl: an architecture description language based on the higher-order typed pi-calculus for
           specifying dynamic and mobile software architectures. *SIGSOFT Softw. Eng. Notes*, pages 1–14, 2004.
[OTK04]   Shougo Ogata, Tatsuhiro Tsuchiya, and Tohru Kikuno. Sat-based verification of safe petri nets. In Farn Wang,
           editor, *Automated Technology for Verification and Analysis*, volume 3299 of *Lecture Notes in Computer Science*,
           pages 79–92. Springer Berlin Heidelberg, 2004.
[RT86]   G. Rozenberg and P.S. Thiagarajan. Petri nets: Basic notions, structure, behaviour. In J.W. Bakker, W.-P.
           Roever, and G. Rozenberg, editors, *Current Trends in Concurrency*, volume 224 of *Lecture Notes in Computer
           Science*, pages 585–668. Springer Berlin Heidelberg, 1986.
[RVMS12]   Fernando Rosa-Velardo and María Martos-Salgado. Multiset rewriting for the verification of depth-bounded
           processes with name binding. *Inf. Comput.*, 215:68–87, June 2012.

[SW01]   Davide Sangiorgi and David Walker. *The Pi-Calculus - a theory of mobile processes.* Cambridge University Press, 2001.

[TZH02]   David Teller, Pascal Zimmer, and Daniel Hirschkoff. Using ambients to control resources*. In Luboš Brim, Mojmír Křetínský, Antonín Kučera, and Petr Jančar, editors, *CONCUR 2002 — Concurrency Theory*, volume 2421 of *Lecture Notes in Computer Science*, pages 288–303. Springer Berlin Heidelberg, 2002.

[UAUC10]   Devrim Unal, Ozan Akar, and M. Ufuk Caglayan. Model checking of location and mobility related security policy specifications in ambient calculus. In Igor Kotenko and Victor Skormin, editors, *Computer Network Security*, volume 6258 of *Lecture Notes in Computer Science*, pages 155–168. Springer Berlin Heidelberg, 2010.

[Val98]   Antti Valmari. The state explosion problem. In *Lectures on Petri Nets I: Basic Models, Advances in Petri Nets, the volumes are based on the Advanced Course on Petri Nets*, pages 429–528, London, UK, UK, 1998. Springer-Verlag.

[WZH10]   Thomas Wies, Damien Zufferey, and Thomas A. Henzinger. Forward analysis of depth-bounded processes. In C.-H. Luke Ong, editor, *FOSSACS*, volume 6014 of *Lecture Notes in Computer Science*, pages 94–108. Springer, 2010.

Printed in the United States
By Bookmasters